■ SCHOLAS

·3

MW00697535

JANUARY
Monthly Idea Book

Ready-to-Use Templates, Activities, Management Tools, and More — for Every Day of the Month

Karen Sevaly

New York • Toronto • London • Auckland • Sydney
Mexico City • New Delhi • Hong Kong • Buenos Aires **Teaching** *Resources*

DEDICATION

This book is dedicated to teachers and children everywhere.

Cover design by Maria Lilja
Cover art by Jillian Phillips
Interior design by Melinda Belter
Illustrations by Karen Sevaly

ISBN 978-0-545-37937-3

1 2 3 4 5 6 7 8 9 10   40   19 18 17 16 15 14 13

CONTENTS

FAVORITE TOPICS

HAPPY NEW YEAR!

CONTENTS

CHINESE NEW YEAR

Reproducible Patterns

DR. MARTIN LUTHER KING, JR.

WINTRY WEATHER

CONTENTS

THE ARCTIC AND ANTARCTIC

Reproducible Patterns

AWARDS, INCENTIVES, AND MORE

INTRODUCTION

Welcome to the original Monthly Idea Book series! This book was written especially for teachers getting ready to teach topics related to the month of January.

Each book in this month-by-month series is filled with dozens of ideas for PreK–3 classrooms. Activities connect to the Common Core State Standards for Reading (Foundational Skills), among other subjects, to help you meet the needs of your students. (For more information, see page 16.)

Most everything you need to prepare the lessons and activities in this resource is included, such as:

- calendar and weather-related props

- book cover patterns and stationery for writing assignments

- booklet patterns

- games and puzzles that support learning in curriculum areas such as math, science, and writing

- activity sheets that help students organize information, respond to learning, and explore topics in a meaningful way

- patterns for projects that connect to holidays, special occasions, and commemorative events

All year long, you can weave the ideas and reproducible patterns in these unique books into your monthly lesson plans and classroom activities. Happy teaching!

What's Inside

You'll find that this book is
chock-full of reproducibles
that make lesson planning easier:

■ puppets and
picture props

■ bookmarks,
booklets, and
book covers

■ game boards,
puzzles, and
word finds

■ stationery

■ awards and certificates

How to Use This Book

The reproducible pages in this book have flexible use and may be modified to meet your particular classroom needs. Use the reproducible activity pages and patterns in conjunction with the suggested activities or weave them into your curriculum in other ways.

★ PHOTOCOPY OR SCAN

To get started, think about your developing lesson plans and upcoming bulletin boards. If desired, carefully remove the pages you will need. Duplicate those pages on copy paper, color paper, tagboard, or overhead transparency sheets. If you have access to a scanner, consider saving the pattern pages as PDF files. That way, you can size images up or down and customize them with text to create individualized lessons, center-time activities, interactive whiteboard lessons, homework pages, and more.

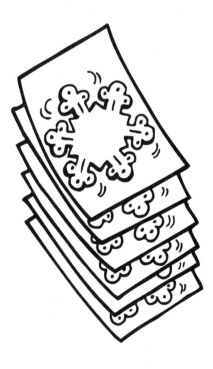

★ LAMINATE FOR DURABILITY

Laminating the reproducibles will help you extend their use. If you have access to a roll laminator, then you already know how fortunate you are when it comes to saving time and resources. If you don't have a laminator, clear adhesive vinyl covering works well. Just sandwich the pattern between two sheets of vinyl and cut off any excess. Then try some of these ideas:

- Put laminated sheets of stationery in a writing center to use for handwriting practice. Wipe-off markers work great on coated pages and can easily be erased with dry tissue.

- Add longevity to calendars, weather-related pictures, and pocket chart rebus pictures by preserving them with lamination.

- Transform picture props into flannel board figures. After lamination, add a tab of hook-and-loop fastener to the back of the props and invite students to adhere them to the flannel board for storytelling fun.

- To enliven magnet board activities, affix sections of magnet tape to the back of the picture props. Then encourage students to sort images according to the skills you're working on. For example, you might have them group images by commonalities such as initial sound, habitat, or physical attributes.

BULLETIN BOARDS

1. Set the Stage

Use background paper colors that complement many themes and seasons. For example, the dark background you used as a spooky display in October will have dramatic effect in November, when you begin a unit on woodland animals or Thanksgiving.

While paper works well, there are other background options available. You might also try fabric from a colorful bed sheet or gingham material. Discontinued rolls of patterned wallpaper can be purchased at discount stores. What's more, newspapers are easy to use and readily available. Attach a background of comics to set off a lesson on riddles, or use grocery store flyers to provide food for thought on a bulletin board about nutrition.

2. Make the Display

The reproducible patterns in this book can be enlarged to fit your needs. When we say enlarge, we mean it! Think BIG! Use an overhead projector to enlarge the images you need to make your bulletin board extraordinary.

If your school has a stencil press, you're lucky. The rest of us can use these strategies for making headers and titles.

- Cut strips of paper, cloud shapes, or cartoon bubbles. They will all look great! Then, by hand, write the text using wide-tipped permanent markers or tempera paint.

- If you must cut individual letters, use 4- by 6-inch pieces of construction paper. (Laminate first, if you can.) Cut the uppercase letters as shown on page 14. No need to measure, as somewhat irregular letters will look creative, not messy.

3. Add Color and Embellishments

Use your imagination! You'll be surprised at the great displays you can create.

- ■ Watercolor markers work great on small areas. On larger areas, you can switch to crayons, color chalk, or pastels. (Lamination will keep the color off of you. No laminator? A little hairspray will do the trick as a fixative.)

- ■ Cut character eyes and teeth from white paper and glue them in place. The features will really stand out and make your bulletin boards engaging.

- ■ For special effects, include items that provide texture and visual interest, such as buttons, yarn, and lace. Try cellophane or blue glitter glue on water scenes. Consider using metallic wrapping paper or aluminum foil to add a bit of shimmer to stars and belt buckles.

- ■ Finally, take a picture of your completed bulletin board. Store the photos in a recipe box or large sturdy envelope. Next year when you want to create the same display, you'll know right where everything goes. You might even want to supply students with pushpins and invite them to recreate the display, following your directions and using the photograph as support.

Staying Organized

Organizing materials with monthly file folders provides you with a location to save reproducible activity pages and patterns, along with related craft ideas, recipes, and magazine or periodical articles.

If you prefer, use file boxes instead of folders. You'll find that with boxes there will plenty of room to store enlarged patterns, sample art projects, bulletin board materials, and much more.

Meeting the Standards

CONNECTIONS TO THE COMMON CORE STATE STANDARDS

The Common Core State Standards Initiative (CCSSI) has outlined learning expectations in English/Language Arts, among other subject areas, for students at different grade levels. In general, the activities in this book align with the following standards for students in grades K–3. For more information, visit the CCSSI website at www.corestandards.org.

Reading: Foundational Skills

Print Concepts
- RF.K.1, RF.1.1. Demonstrate understanding of the organization and basic features of print.

Phonics and Word Recognition
- RF.K.3, RF.1.3, RF.2.3, RF.3.3. Know and apply grade-level phonics and word analysis skills in decoding words.

Fluency
- RF.K.4. Read emergent-reader texts with purpose and understanding.
- RF.1.4, RF.2.4, RF.3.4. Read with sufficient accuracy and fluency to support comprehension.

Writing

Production and Distribution of Writing
- W.3.4. Produce writing in which the development and organization are appropriate to task and purpose.
- W.K.5, W.1.5, W.2.5, W.3.5. Focus on a topic and strengthen writing as needed by revising and editing.

Research to Build and Present Knowledge
- W.K.7, W.1.7, W.2.7. Participate in shared research and writing projects.
- W.3.7. Conduct short research projects that build knowledge about a topic.
- W.K.8, W.1.8, W.2.8, W.3.8. Recall information from experiences or gather information from provided sources to answer a question.

Range of Writing
- W.3.10. Write routinely over extended time frames (time for research, reflection, and revision) and shorter time frames (a single sitting or a day or two) for a range of discipline-specific tasks, purposes, and audiences.

Speaking & Listening

Comprehension and Collaboration
- SL.K.1, SL.1.1, SL.2.1. Participate in collaborative conversations with diverse partners about grade-level topics and texts with peers and adults in small and larger groups.
- SL.K.2, SL.1.2, SL.2.2, SL.3.2. Recount or describe key ideas or details from a text read aloud or information presented orally or through other media.
- SL.K.3, SL.1.3, SL.2.3, SL.3.3. Ask and answer questions about what a speaker says in order to gather additional information or clarify something that is not understood.

Presentation of Knowledge and Ideas
- SL.K.4, SL.1.4, SL.2.4. Describe people, places, things, and events with relevant details, expressing ideas and feelings clearly.
- SL.K.5, SL.1.5, SL.2.5, SL.3.5. Add drawings or other visual displays to stories or recounts of experiences when appropriate to clarify ideas, thoughts, and feelings.

Language

Conventions of Standard English
- L.K.1, L.1.1, L.2.1, L.3.1. Demonstrate command of the conventions of standard English grammar and usage when writing or speaking.
- L.K.2, L.1.2, L.2.2, L.3.2. Demonstrate command of the conventions of standard English capitalization, punctuation, and spelling when writing.

Knowledge of Language
- L.2.3, L.3.3. Use knowledge of language and its conventions when writing, speaking, reading, or listening.

Vocabulary Acquisition and Use
- L.K.4, L.1.4, L.2.4, L.3.4. Determine or clarify the meaning of unknown and multiple-meaning words and phrases based on grade level reading and content, choosing flexibly from an array of strategies.
- L.K.6, L.1.6, L.2.6, L.3.6. Use words and phrases acquired through conversations, reading and being read to, and responding to texts.

CALENDAR TIME

Getting Started

January

Sunday	Monday	Tuesday	Wednesday	Thursday	Friday	Saturday

19

CALENDAR

★ MARK YOUR CALENDAR

Make photocopies of the calendar grid on page 19 and use it to meet your needs. Consider using the write-on spaces to:

- write the corresponding numerals for each day

- mark and count how many days have passed

- track the weather with stamps or stickers

- note student birthdays

- record homework assignments

- communicate with families about positive behaviors

- remind volunteers about schedules, field trips, shortened days, and so on

CELEBRATIONS THIS MONTH

Whether you post a photocopy of pages 20 though 23 near your class calendar or just turn to these pages for inspiration, you're sure to find lots of information on them to discuss with students. To take celebrating and learning a step further, invite the class to add more to the list. For example, students can add anniversaries of significant events and the birthdays of their favorite authors or historical figures.

CALENDAR HEADER

You can make a photocopy of the header on page 24, color it, and use it as a title for your classroom calendar. You might opt to give the coloring job to a student who has a birthday that month. The student is sure to enjoy seeing his or her artwork each and every day of the month.

BEFORE INTRODUCING WHAT'S THE WEATHER?

Make a photocopy of the body template on page 25. Laminate it so you can use it again and again. Before sharing the template with the class, cut out pieces of cloth in the shapes of clothing students typically wear this month. For example, if you live in a warm weather climate, your January attire might include shorts and t-shirts. If you live in chillier climates, your attire might include a scarf, hat, and coat. Fit the cutouts to the body outline. When the clothing props are made, and you're ready to have students dress the template, display the clothing. Invite the "weather helper of the day" to tell what pieces of clothing he or she would choose to dress appropriately for the weather. (For extra fun, use foam to cut out accessories such as an umbrella, sunhat, and raincoat.

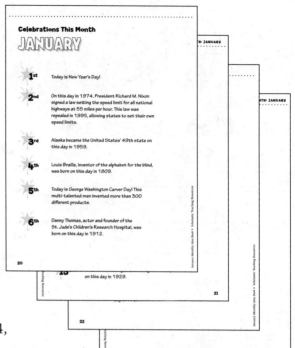

January

Sunday	Monday	Tuesday	Wednesday	Thursday	Friday	Saturday

Celebrations This Month

JANUARY

1st Today is New Year's Day!

2nd On this day in 1974, President Richard M. Nixon signed a law setting the speed limit for all national highways at 55 miles per hour. This law was repealed in 1995, allowing states to set their own speed limits.

3rd Alaska became the United States' 49th state on this day in 1959.

4th Louis Braille, inventor of the alphabet for the blind, was born on this day in 1809.

5th Today is George Washington Carver Day! This multi-talented man invented more than 300 different products.

6th Danny Thomas, actor and founder of the St. Jude's Children's Research Hospital, was born on this day in 1912.

January Monthly Idea Book © Scholastic Teaching Resources

7th Millard Fillmore, the 13th President of the United States, was born on this day in 1800.

8th Elvis Presley, an American music icon, was born on this day in 1935.

9th On this day in 1493, Christopher Columbus reported seeing mermaids, but the creatures he observed were actually manatees!

10th "Black Gold," also known as oil, was discovered in Texas on this day in 1901.

11th On this day in 1908, President Theodore Roosevelt made the Grand Canyon a national monument.

12th Jack London, author of *Call of the Wild*, was born on this day in 1876.

13th Michael Bond, author of the Paddington Bear series, was born on this day in 1926.

14th Albert Schweitzer, a humanitarian and 1952 Nobel Peace Prize recipient, was born on this day in 1875.

15th Martin Luther King, Jr., a civil rights leader, was born on this day in 1929.

16th Andre Michelin, born on this day in 1853, founded a company that manufactured inflatable, removable tires for bikes and cars.

17th Benjamin Franklin, a statesman and inventor, was born on this day in 1706.

18th Muhammad Ali, an American heavyweight boxing champion and social activist, was born on this day in 1942.

19th Robert E. Lee, General of the Confederate Army during the Civil War, was born on this day in 1807.

20th Today is Presidential Inauguration Day in the United States.

21st The *USS Nautilus*, the world's first nuclear submarine was launched to sea on this day in 1955.

22nd Rafe Martin, storyteller and author of *The Rough-Face Girl*, was born on this day in 1946.

23rd John Hancock, an American patriot and signer of the Declaration of Independence, was born on this day in 1737.

24th Gold was discovered in Sutter's Mill, California, on this day in 1848.

25th The world's largest diamond was found in South Africa on this day in 1905.

26th On this day in 2005, Condoleeza Rice became the first black woman to serve as the U. S. Secretary of State.

27th Wolfgang Amadeus Mozart, the famous Austrian composer, was born on this day in 1756.

28th The United States Coast Guard was established on this day in 1915.

29th Rosemary Wells, author of the Max and Ruby book series, was born on this day in 1943.

30th Franklin Delano Roosevelt, 32nd President of the United States and founder of the *March of Dimes*, was born on this day in 1922.

31st Jackie Robinson, the first black Major League baseball player, was born on this day in 1919.

January

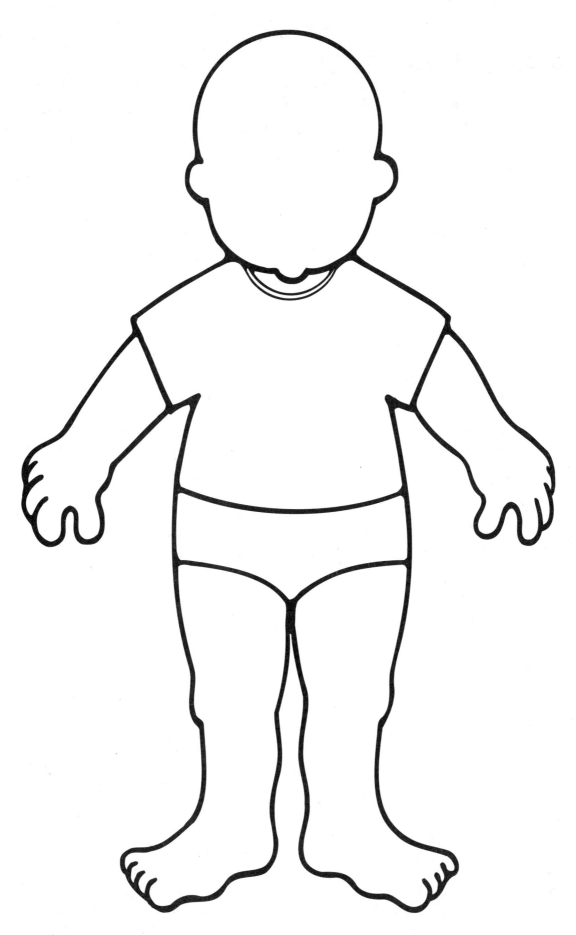

HAPPY NEW YEAR!

People around the world celebrate the start of a new year in different ways. Here are a few traditions from around the globe to share with students:

United States

For most people in the United States, New Year's Eve is celebrated on December 31st. It includes lots of revelry and toasts to friends, both old and new. The next day, the first day of January, is marked by less boisterous celebrations. It is a day when people reflect on the past year and make resolutions, or promises to better themselves in some way.

For some Americans, the old year is symbolized by Father Time and the New Year is represented by a baby in diapers. For others, when and how they celebrate the New Year is prescribed by cultural traditions distinct to a region or heritage.

- In some communities in the southern United States, it is customary to eat certain foods on New Year's Day. Along with eating black-eyed peas to symbolize pennies, some southerners also eat greens to represent dollar bills in hopes of bringing prosperity through the coming year.

- Peoples of the Seminole nation, who live primarily in Florida and Oklahoma, celebrate the harvest of new corn as the beginning of the New Year. This event occurs over four days in the month of July.

Israel

The Jewish New Year, also called Rosh Hashanah, provides a quiet time for meditation and prayer. This is a holy time for the Jewish people, considered by them to be the birthday of the world. Each person asks forgiveness from God and vows to live a better life. Rosh Hashanah is celebrated on the first day of the Jewish calendar, usually in September or October.

China

Chinese New Year is the first day of the new moon using the Chinese lunar calendar. It falls sometime between the middle of January and early March. This holiday is celebrated for about two weeks. It marks the beginning of a new cycle of life and symbolizes both the end of winter and the coming of spring. For more information about this holiday, turn to page 54.

Nigeria

The people in northern Nigeria celebrate the new year at the beginning of fishing season, usually the first part of February. Thousands gather along the banks of the Sokoto River with fish nets in hand. On a signal, everyone jumps in the water, startling the fish into the nets. The fisherman who catches the largest fish wins a prize.

Germany

The people of Germany and a few other European nations have a custom called "lead pouring." On New Year's Day, people put hot drops of melted lead into containers of cold water. As the lead cools and hardens, unusual shapes appear. People have fun telling their fortunes by the shapes of the lead. According to custom, if the lead shape resembles a coin, they might look forward to obtaining money.

> Silvester is another name for New Year's Eve in many European countries, including Austria, Poland, and Italy. For an extra challenge, ask students to match these spellings with the corresponding languages: *szilveszter, Sylvester,* and *sylwester.*

Suggested Activities

The calendar that most of the world uses today is called the Gregorian Calendar, named after Pope Gregory XIII, who declared its use in 1582. The Gregorian calendar is based upon the time it takes for the earth to make one complete revolution around the sun, which is 365 days, 5 hours and 48 minutes. The extra minutes eventually add up to an extra day. So, every four years we add it to the end of the month of February (Leap Year).

 ## FUN WITH WORD FINDS

Start the year out right with the word finds (pages 32 and 33) that feature words associated with the New Year's holiday and the months of the year. Students will search for words they most likely have encountered over their winter vacation as well as a few unfamiliar words, too. After students complete the activities and check their work, invite them to brainstorm more words related to the themes of the word finds. Then take vocabulary building a step further by displaying the words from the puzzle word banks and the words students brainstormed on a class word wall. Invite students to visit the word wall to get inspiration for their New Year's creative writing assignments.

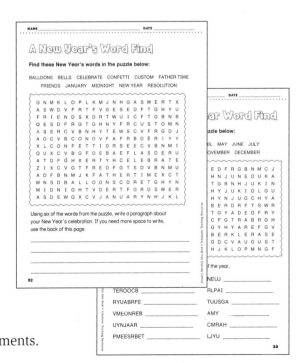

HELP DREAMS COME TRUE!

Use this idea to kick off a New Year's fundraiser for a charitable organization dedicated to helping children. Enlist the help of your students in saving pennies for a worthy charity. (A penny isn't much, but students will learn that when they work together, they can save enough pennies to make a worthwhile contribution.) Before you start this activity, notify families of the upcoming activity and secure a safe place to store rolled pennies in the classroom or school office. As students collect the pennies, you'll find many opportunities to use them for practicing math skills, such as counting, creating sets, and adding. This activity also provides a meaningful way to teach about the joy of sharing and giving. Here are a few charitable organizations to consider for your donation:

- The Make-a-Wish Foundation of America literally makes wishes come true for children with life-threatening medical conditions: www.wish.org

- Teach for America provides children who live in low-income communities with teachers dedicated to eliminating inequities in education: www.teachforamerica.org

- Save the Children is dedicated to helping children and families around the world help themselves, and to saving lives with food, medical care, and education: www.savethechildren.org

 ## PLEDGES TO BE BETTER

During New Year's celebrations, we often pledge to make the coming year better than the last. Many people make New Year's resolutions. Help students think about ways in which they can be better students, sons or daughters, sisters or brothers, and friends. Distribute photocopies of page 34 and have students complete their page independently. Then ask volunteers to share their pledges for the new year.

NAME _____ DATE _____

My New Year's Resolutions

Think of some resolutions you want to make. Write them below.

Write a resolution for becoming a better . . .

Student _____
_____

Son or Daughter _____
_____

Sister or Brother _____
_____

Friend _____
_____

If every person in the world could be better at just one thing, what should it be?

_____
_____
_____
_____

34

★ NEW YEAR'S VISOR

Make tagboard photocopies of the visor pattern (page 35) to distribute to students along with scissors, hole-punches, and 10-inch lengths of elasticized string. Explain that students will make visors to help usher in the new year. To assemble, have students:

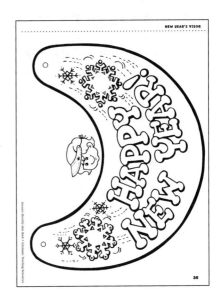

1. Color and cut out the visor pattern.

2. Punch a hole at each end of the visor, where indicated.

3. Tie one end of the elasticized string to each hole. (With elasticized string, students can easily remove their visors without retying.)

★ DESKTOP CALENDAR

Invite students to make this calendar to use as a desk reference. To get started, provide them with tagboard photocopies of the calendar patterns (pages 36–38), scissors, three brass fasteners, a hole-punch, and crayons or markers for decorating the calendars. Then have them do the following to make their calendar:

1. Cut out the calendar cover and wheels.

2. Write the year on the cover. (If desired, add colorful designs and your name to personalize it.)

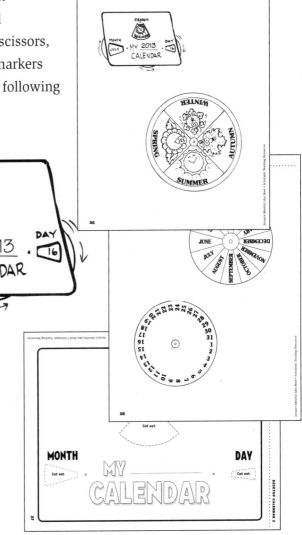

3. Carefully cut out the openings on the cover to create windows. (Younger students may need assistance with this.)

4. Punch a hole, where indicated, near each window cutout.

5. Use the brass fasteners to attach the wheels to the back of the cover. Check that each wheel is in the appropriate place and that the season, month, or number appears in the window as the wheel is turned.

29

MY BOOK OF MONTHS

Launch the new year with a booklet dedicated to learning and thinking about the twelve months of the year. To start, show students a typical calendar. As you go through each month, ask volunteers to help answer questions about how many days are in the month, words that describe the month, and favorite holidays, events, or things to do in that month. Then distribute photocopies of pages 39–51 to the class, so that each student has a complete set of pages. Have students:

1. Write their responses to complete each page of their booklets. Color the art, if desired.

2. Trade papers with a partner to help check spelling.

3. Correct their pages, then sequence them by months.

4. Staple the pages behind the cover.

★ WHEN YOU WISH UPON A STAR . . . .

To prepare for this activity, cover a bulletin board with dark blue or black paper. Title the board "When You Wish Upon a Star . . ." When ready, give students photocopies of the star on page 52. Explain that you'd like them to record their wishes for the year ahead. Attach the stars to a bulletin board for display. At the end of the school year, return the stars to each student along with a note that expresses your wishes for him or her and your hopes that the child's dreams come true.

★ YEARLY FAVORITES BOOKS

Invite students to think about their favorite time of the year. It could be a month, a season, or a particular day of the year. Ask them to write about it in the form of a poem or short story. Distribute photocopies of the bell-shaped book cover on page 53 for students to use when they are ready to publish their writing.

A New Year's Word Find

Find these New Year's words in the puzzle below:

BALLOONS   BELLS   CELEBRATE   CONFETTI   CUSTOM   FATHER TIME
FRIENDS   JANUARY   MIDNIGHT   NEW YEAR   RESOLUTION

```
G N M K L O P L K M J N H G A S W E R T X
A S W D V F R T F V G E S E D F T G H Y U
F R I E N D S X D R T W U I C F T G B N B
Q E S D F R G T G H N Y F R C U S T O M N
A S E R C V B N H Y T E W S C V F R G D J
A O C V B C O N D V F A F R B D E R T Y Y
X L C O N F E T T I D R S E E C V B N M I
Q U X C V B G F D E B A E F L A S D E R U
A T D F G H X E R T Y H C E L E B R A T E
Z I X C V G T F R E D F G T S D V B N M U
A O F B N M J K F A T H E R T I M E X C T
W N S D B A L L O O N S C D R E T G H Y N
M I D N I G H T V D E R T F G R D S W E R
A S D E W Q X C V J A N U A R Y N H J K L
```

Using six of the words from the puzzle, write a paragraph about your New Year's celebration. If you need more space to write, use the back of this page.

_____

_____

_____

_____

January Monthly Idea Book © Scholastic Teaching Resources

Months-of-the-Year Word Find

Find the names of the months in the puzzle below:

JANUARY   FEBRUARY   MARCH   APRIL   MAY   JUNE   JULY
AUGUST   SEPTEMBER   OCTOBER   NOVEMBER   DECEMBER

```
A  M  S  D  F  R  E  T  G  D  C  Q  A  S  E  D  F  R  G  B  N  M  C  J
A  X  C  M  A  R  C  H  A  C  F  V  B  G  H  N  J  U  N  E  O  U  K  A
A  B  S  D  E  F  R  T  G  J  S  D  E  R  T  G  B  N  H  J  U  K  I  N
P  S  D  S  E  P  T  E  M  B  E  R  F  G  H  Y  J  U  K  I  O  L  G  U
R  D  F  G  T  H  Y  J  U  D  F  R  T  G  H  Y  N  J  U  G  C  H  Y  A
I  S  W  E  D  C  V  G  T  D  E  C  E  M  B  E  R  D  R  F  T  S  W  R
L  S  X  C  V  B  G  F  D  S  A  W  E  R  T  G  Y  A  D  E  O  F  R  Y
X  S  A  F  R  E  T  Y  H  G  T  R  E  D  C  F  G  T  R  A  B  R  G  H
G  J  U  L  Y  A  X  M  Z  S  E  R  C  V  G  Y  H  Y  A  R  E  F  G  V
X  Z  C  V  B  G  T  A  A  N  O  V  E  M  B  E  R  K  L  E  R  A  S  E
A  W  S  D  F  R  C  Y  A  S  D  C  V  F  G  D  C  V  A  U  G  U  S  T
A  S  X  F  E  B  R  U  A  R  Y  C  V  B  H  J  K  L  O  P  M  N  G  F
```

Unscramble the letters to spell the months of the year.

BDREECEM _____   NEUJ _____

TEROOCB _____   RLPAI _____

RYUABRFE _____   TUUSGA _____

VMEONREB _____   AMY _____

UYNJAAR _____   CMRAH _____

PMEESRBET _____   LJYU _____

My New Year's Resolutions

Think of some resolutions you want to make.
Write them below.

Write a resolution for becoming a better . . .

Student _____

_____

Son or Daughter _____

_____

Sister or Brother _____

_____

Friend _____

_____

If every person in the world could be better at just one thing, what should it be?

_____

_____

_____

_____

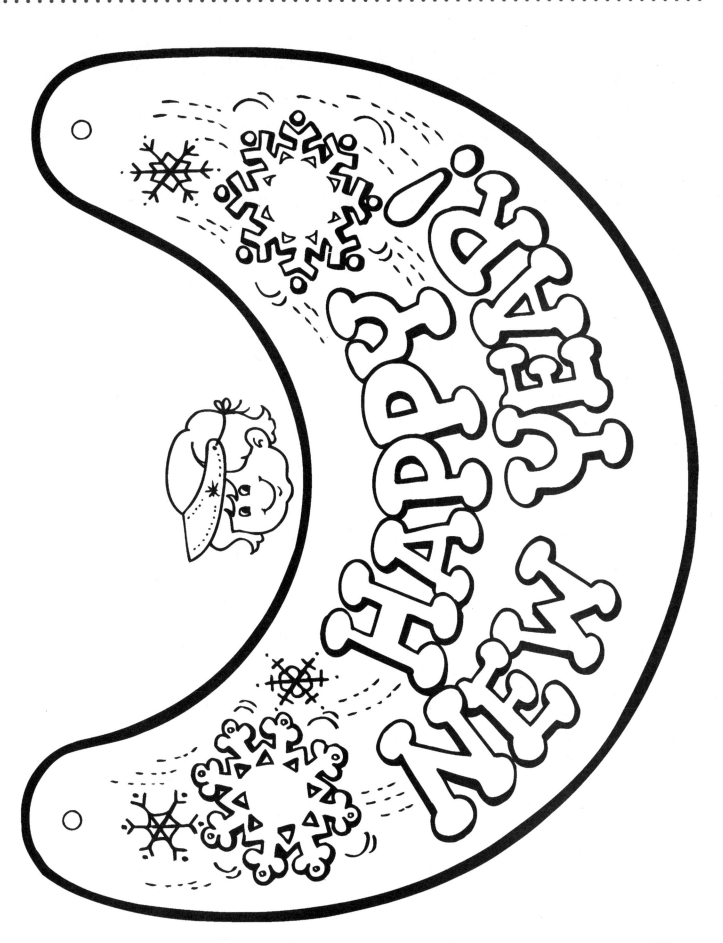

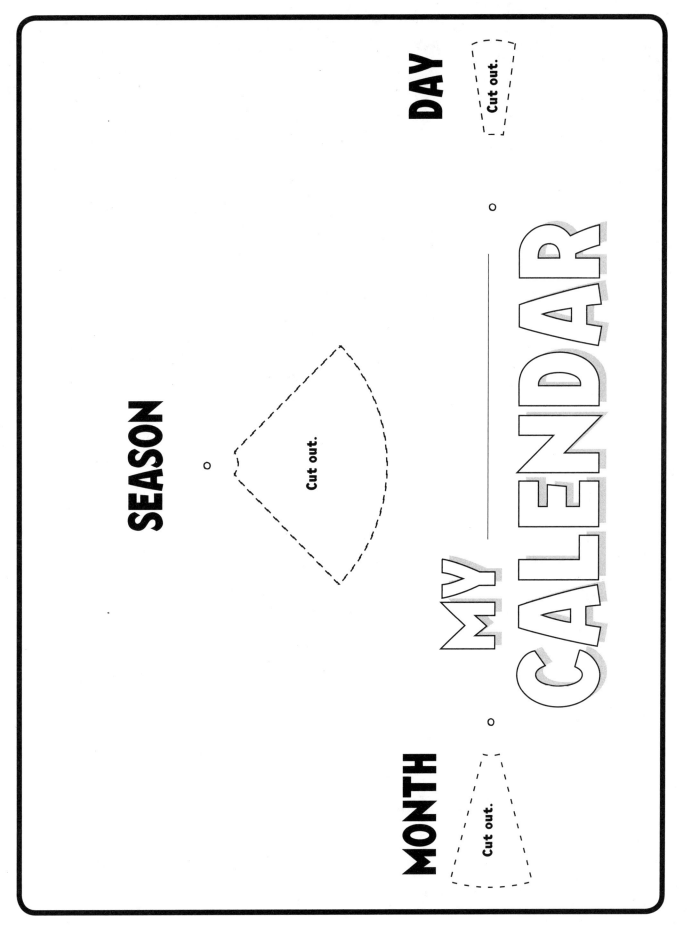

DAY

Cut out.

SEASON

Cut out.

MY
CALENDAR

MONTH

Cut out.

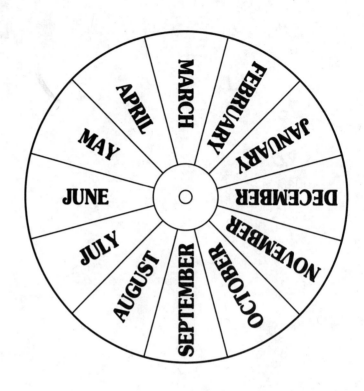

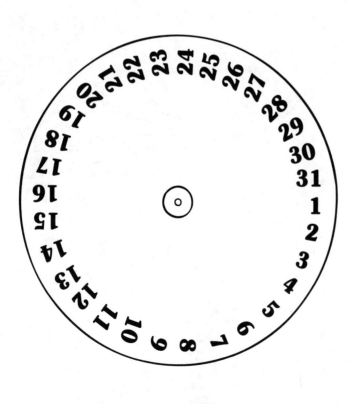

My Book
of Months

Name

January

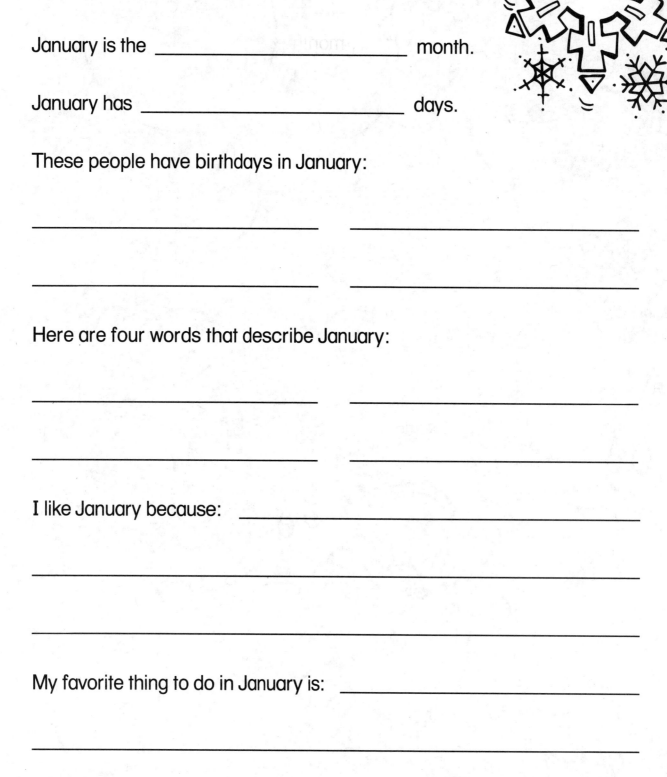

January is the _____ month.

January has _____ days.

These people have birthdays in January:

_____   _____

_____   _____

Here are four words that describe January:

_____   _____

_____   _____

I like January because: _____

_____

_____

My favorite thing to do in January is: _____

_____

February

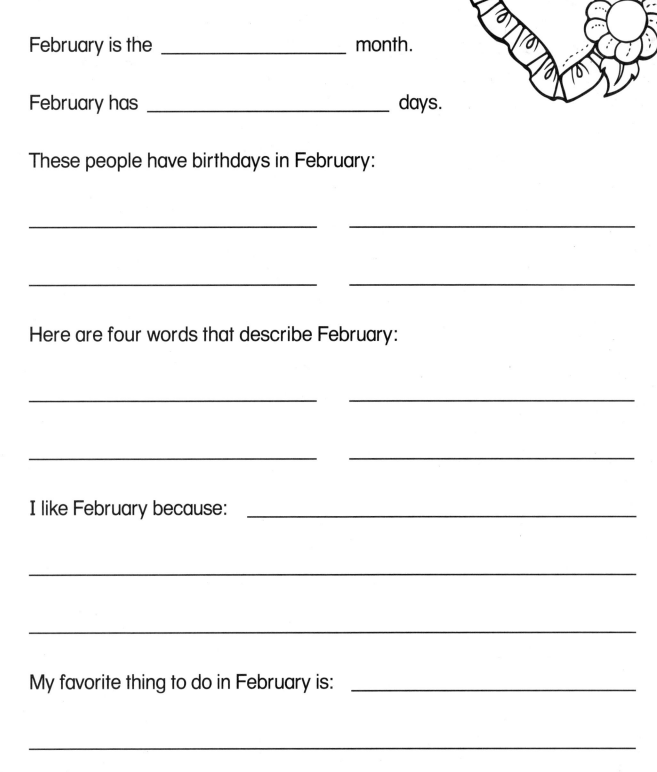

February is the _____ month.

February has _____ days.

These people have birthdays in February:

_____   _____

_____   _____

Here are four words that describe February:

_____   _____

_____   _____

I like February because: _____

_____

_____

My favorite thing to do in February is: _____

_____

March

March is the _____ month.

March has _____ days.

These people have birthdays in March:

_____   _____

_____   _____

Here are four words that describe March:

_____   _____

_____   _____

I like March because: _____

_____

_____

My favorite thing to do in March is: _____

_____

April

April is the _____ month.

April has _____ days.

These people have birthdays in April:

_____   _____

_____   _____

Here are four words that describe April:

_____   _____

_____   _____

I like April because: _____

_____

_____

My favorite thing to do in April is: _____

_____

May

May is the _____ month.

May has _____ days.

These people have birthdays in May:

_____   _____

_____   _____

Here are four words that describe May:

_____   _____

_____   _____

I like May because: _____

_____

_____

My favorite thing to do in May is: _____

_____

June

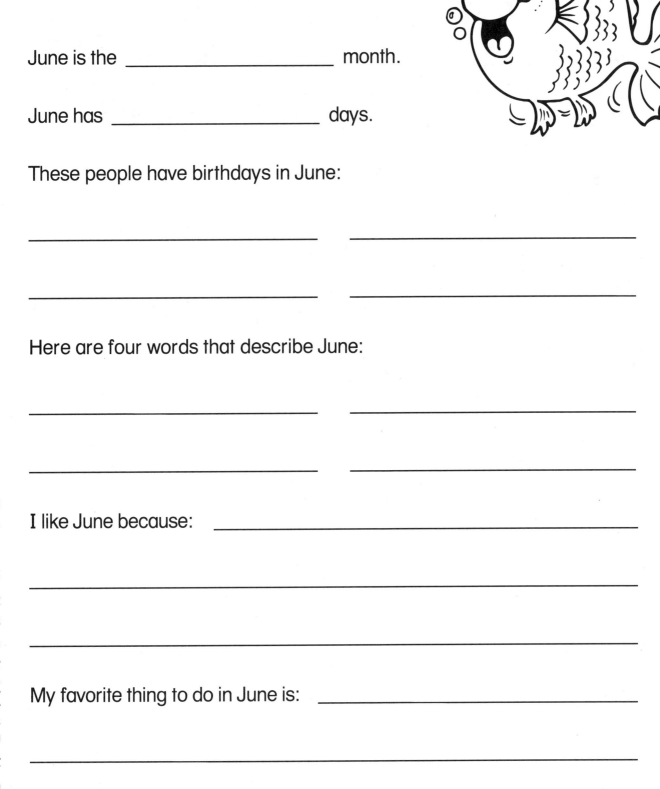

June is the _____ month.

June has _____ days.

These people have birthdays in June:

_____   _____

_____   _____

Here are four words that describe June:

_____   _____

_____   _____

I like June because: _____

_____

_____

My favorite thing to do in June is: _____

_____

July

July is the _____ month.

July has _____ days.

These people have birthdays in July:

_____   _____

_____   _____

Here are four words that describe July:

_____   _____

_____   _____

I like July because: _____

_____

_____

My favorite thing to do in July is: _____

_____

August

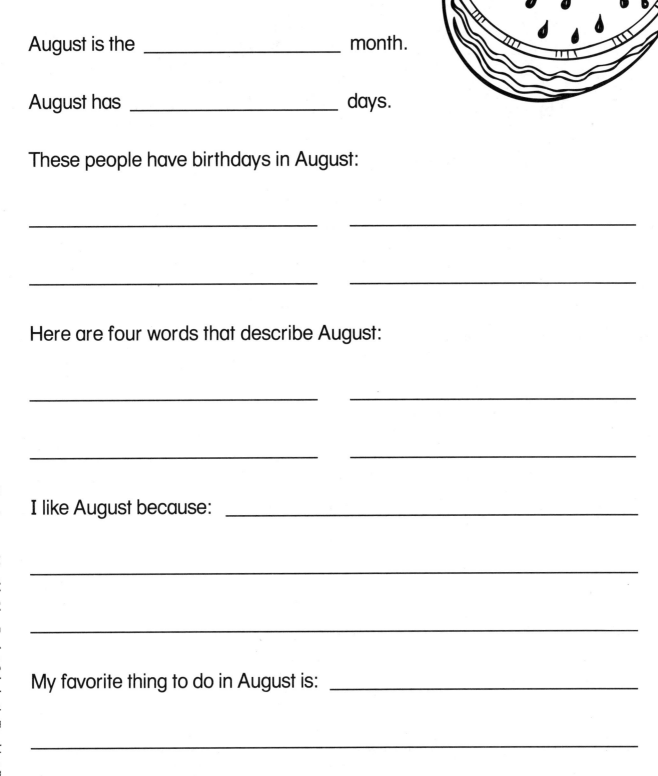

August is the _____ month.

August has _____ days.

These people have birthdays in August:

_____   _____

_____   _____

Here are four words that describe August:

_____   _____

_____   _____

I like August because: _____

_____

_____

My favorite thing to do in August is: _____

_____

September

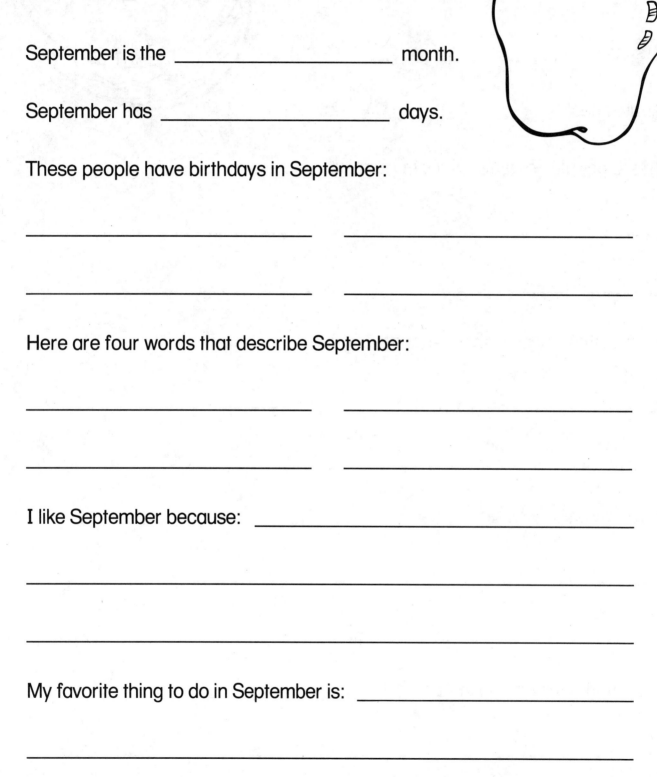

September is the _____ month.

September has _____ days.

These people have birthdays in September:

_____   _____

_____   _____

Here are four words that describe September:

_____   _____

_____   _____

I like September because: _____

_____

_____

My favorite thing to do in September is: _____

_____

October

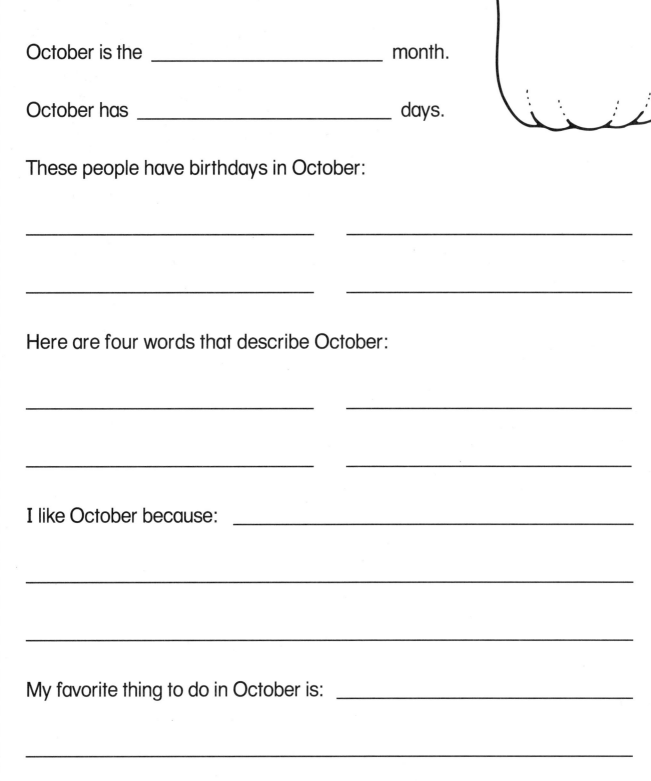

October is the _____ month.

October has _____ days.

These people have birthdays in October:

_____   _____

_____   _____

Here are four words that describe October:

_____   _____

_____   _____

I like October because: _____

_____

_____

My favorite thing to do in October is: _____

_____

November

November is the _____ month.

November has _____ days.

These people have birthdays in November:

_____   _____

_____   _____

Here are four words that describe November:

_____   _____

_____   _____

I like November because: _____

_____

_____

My favorite thing to do in November is: _____

_____

December

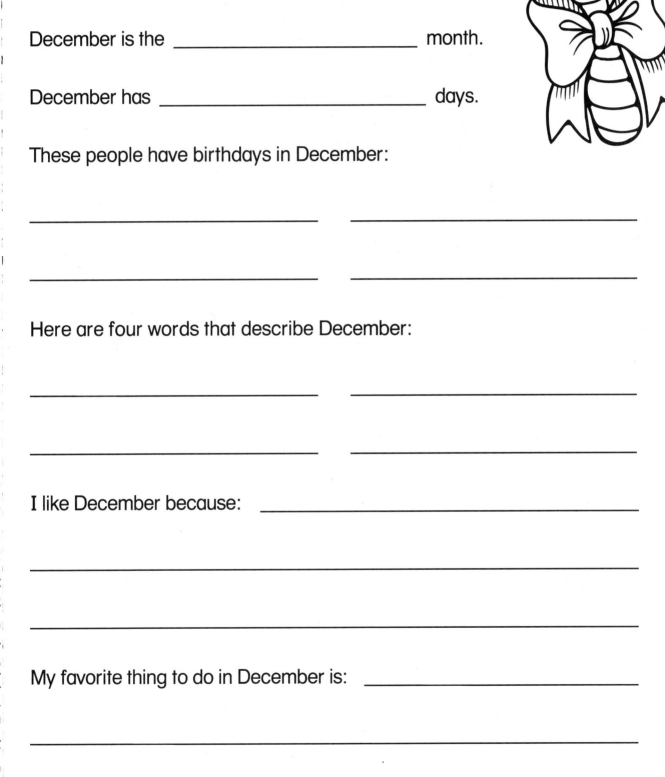

December is the _____ month.

December has _____ days.

These people have birthdays in December:

_____   _____

_____   _____

Here are four words that describe December:

_____   _____

_____   _____

I like December because: _____

_____

_____

My favorite thing to do in December is: _____

_____

January Monthly Idea Book © Scholastic Teaching Resources

PLACE THIS SIDE ALONG FOLD.

January Monthly Idea Book © Scholastic Teaching Resources

CHINESE NEW YEAR

For the Chinese, the 15-day New Year celebration is perhaps the most colorful and joyous event of the year. It includes days of preparation and weeks of rejoicing.

Preparation

The last days of the old year are busy, as all of the food for the celebrations must be prepared in advance. It is considered bad luck to use a knife or sharp tool during the first few days of the New Year, for fear of "cutting" the New Year's luck. All debts must be paid and accounting books brought up to date before the end of the year. Cleaning the house is especially important during this time. Then, on the eve of the Chinese New Year, the outer door to the house is sealed with red paper to prevent good luck from leaving the house.

New Year's Day

The entire family gathers for a feast of rice pudding, vegetarian dishes, and pastries. The New Year marks the birthday of every family member. Before midnight, children receive good luck money in even-numbered amounts, wrapped in small red envelopes. Everyone wears their newest clothes, and only kind words are to be thought or spoken.

Feast of Lanterns

On the third day of the New Year, lanterns of all shapes, sizes, and colors decorate streets and homes. Many cities host parades led by a dragon, a symbol of good luck. Made of bamboo and covered with silk and paper, the dragon may be supported by more than fifty people as it weaves up and down the streets. Musicians, dancers, and acrobats accompany the dragon in the parade. A fireworks display signifies the end of the celebration.

Suggested Activities

 ## CHINESE NEW YEAR BANNER

Children will enjoy speaking and writing Chinese as part of their Chinese New Year celebration. Ask students to pronounce the words "Xīn Nián Kuài Lè" (shing nian kwai ler), which means "Happy New Year." After students have perfected their greetings, challenge them to try writing the characters "Xīn Nián Kuài Lè."

You can distribute photocopies of page 60 for them to use as a model. As students write, remind them to copy the characters in order vertically.

To make Chinese New Year banners, provide students with red construction paper, yarn, and other craft supplies. Have them cut out and glue their Chinese characters to the construction paper. For a hanger, help each student tape a 12-inch length of yarn to the top corners of his or her banner. Students can then take their banners home to hang on a wall or door.

★ FESTIVAL LANTERN

Make dozens of Chinese lanterns to hang on strings around the classroom. They're sure to create a festive atmosphere for any New Year celebration. To get started, give a photocopy of the pattern on page 61 to each student. If you made photocopies on white paper, invite students to color the lantern with markers or brightly colored pastels. When ready, have students:

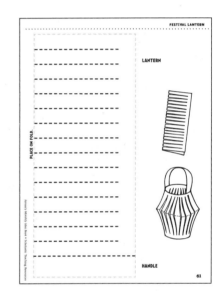

1. Fold their patterns in half and cut along the lines as shown.

2. Unfold the paper and bring the two short edges together to form a cylinder. Staple in place.

3. Add the paper handle. (Or use yarn for the handle.)

★ CHINESE ZODIAC

The Chinese zodiac is based on the phases of the moon and is made up of 12 yearly cycles. Each year is named after an animal. The Chinese believe that a person born in a particular year has the attributes of the animal for that year. Invite students to make a Chinese zodiac by cutting out the patterns on pages 62–65. Then have them arrange the wedge-shaped patterns around the circle and glue the pieces to a sheet of construction paper. The animals should follow this order around the circle: Dragon, Snake, Horse, Ram, Monkey, Rooster, Dog, Pig, Rat, Ox, Tiger, and Hare. When finished, invite students to locate their birth year and decide whether the characteristics shown for that animal reflect their own personalities.

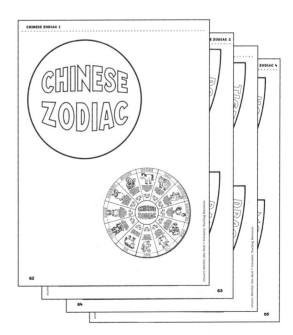

★ A NEW YEAR'S DRAGON

According to Chinese legend, the dragon is a symbol of goodness and strength. Students can make New Year's dragons for a parade using a few simple materials. To get started, divide the class into three or four groups. Provide each group with two large cardboard boxes, brightly colored construction paper, bulletin board paper, paint and paintbrushes, and other craft-making supplies to use for embellishments, such as glitter, foil, and sequins. To make the dragon, ask students to:

1. Cover one box with construction paper to make the dragon's head.

2. Cut the other box in half, and cover each half with construction paper. Then insert the two halves into the open end of the first box to form the dragon's mouth, as shown. Tape or glue the boxes in place.

3. Cut two long sections of bulletin board paper for the dragon's body. (The body should be long enough to cover all of the students who will support the dragon during the parade.)

4. For the spine, cut a strip of paper as long as the body. Cut scallops, zigzags, or fringe along one long edge of the strip. Then glue the two body sections together, trapping the paper spine between them along the top edges and leaving the bottom edges open (as shown above).

5. Attach the body to the head. Trim the other end to resemble a tail. Then use craft items to add facial features and other embellishments to the dragon.

When all of the dragons are complete, invite the class to parade their dragons down the hall, on the playground, or another area at school. Students who are not involved in the procession might ring bells or tap tambourines, providing music for the parade.

★ DRAGON BOARD GAME

Create your own game using this versatile game board. The game can be used for a small-group or learning center activity. Or, make several games and divide the class into groups so they can play at the same time! To get started, photocopy the game boards (pages 66–67). Glue the two parts of the game board together on poster board or to the inside of a file folder. How you use the game and which skills you want students to practice is up to you. Simply write the desired text (or problems) on the spaces of the game board and create task cards to use with the game. Then color the game board and laminate it for durability.

★ GOOD FORTUNE COOKIES

Chinese fortune cookies are fun and easy to make! To begin, ask each student to write a fortune or saying on a small strip of paper and fold it in half. Explain that later each child will select a cookie and read the special fortune written by a fellow classmate. Then invite students to help you make the cookies, following these step-by-step directions:

MATERIALS
Conventional oven • Measuring cup Measuring spoons • Mixing bowl Mixing spoon • Cookie sheet • Timer Spatula • Waxed paper

STEP 1

Gather the following ingredients:

8 egg whites

2 cups sugar

1 cup melted butter

1 cup flour

1 teaspoon vanilla

½ teaspoon salt

4 tablespoons water

STEP 2

Separate egg whites and beat until they form stiff peaks. Blend in the sugar and butter. Add the flour, vanilla, salt, and water and mix until smooth. Spoon the batter into 3-inch circles onto a greased cookie sheet. Bake at 375° F for about 3 minutes.

STEP 3

Use a spatula to move the cookie to waxed paper. Place a fortune in the center of each cookie and gently fold the cookie in half. (If the cookies become difficult to bend, put them back in the oven to warm.)

★ GOOD LUCK NOTES

Invite students to make and share their own good luck wishes for the new year. First, distribute red photocopies of page 68 to students. Ask them to cut out the square-shaped envelope and turn it over to write a message on the back. Next, have students fold the four corners toward the center of the square to cover their message, as shown. (There will be a Chinese symbol on each corner flap.) Finally, have students affix a sticker to hold the flaps in place.

57

★ TANGRAM PUZZLE

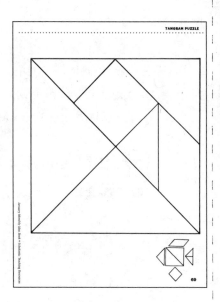

An ancient type of Chinese puzzle is the tangram, which consists of five triangles, a parallelogram, and a small square. These seven shapes can be combined to form many different shapes and designs. Distribute photocopies of the pattern on page 69 for students to cut out. Then have them arrange the tangram pieces into recognizable shapes (such as an animal, building, or scene). When students are ready, have them glue the shapes in place on a sheet of construction paper. Invite volunteers to share the shapes they made with the class.

★ DRAGON PUPPET

Some folks thought that dinosaur bones belonged to dragons. Legends about dragons have fascinated children for centuries. Capitalize on students' interest in dragons with this paper-bag puppet. First, distribute photocopies of the puppet patterns (pages 70–71) for students to color and cut out. (You may want to reduce the patterns for this activity.) Then ask them to glue the dragon's head onto the flat bottom section of a paper bag and its claws along the open edge of the bag. When completed, invite students to use their puppets to perform skits, tell dragon stories, or share what they've learned about the role of dragons in Chinese New Year celebrations.

★ TRADITIONAL DRESS PUPPETS

Divide the class into several groups. Explain that each group will research different aspects of Chinese life and then present their findings to the class. Assign one topic (such as food, clothing, shelter, industry, art, or transportation) to each group to research. Students can use books available in the classroom as well as library books, Internet resources, and other sources such as videos and personal interviews for their research. Tell groups that they should look for information about life in China, both in the past and today, to compare how the people and culture have changed with the times. Younger students will enjoy hearing you read aloud from level-appropriate books on their topic. Afterward, they can discuss the information and then write and/or draw about what they have learned.

Most groups will need a few days to complete this assignment. To help students prepare their presentations, provide copies of the puppet patterns on pages 72–73 for them to cut out, color, and embellish with craft items. For example, students might glue cloth to their puppets to represent traditional formal dress. They can glue wide craft sticks to their puppets to serve as handles. To extend the activity, have groups create posters to show what they've learned about their particular topic. Then invite students to use their puppets and posters to present their findings to the class.

★ DRAGON STATIONERY

Liven up writing assignments with stationery ideal for writing about the Chinese New Year, Chinese culture, lucky dragons, or any other related topic. Distribute several copies of the stationery on page 74 to each student. When students are ready to publish their writing, have them create book covers for their writing project. Then invite volunteers to share their writing with the group.

★ DRAMATIC DISPLAYS

To create an eye-catching heading for a fantastic bulletin board display, use the alphabet letter cards on pages 75–81. Decide on a display title, such as "Fantastic Work on Parade!" Then, photocopy and cut out the letters you need for the title, and arrange them across the top of the bulletin board. Attach students' work to complete the display.

If desired, create a dragon to go along with your stylized title. To do this, enlarge the dragon head (page 70) and several pairs of claws (page 71). Then attach a line of construction paper to the head to make a long, winding dragon body, as shown. Add the pairs of claws in intervals along the body. Finally, attach student work to the sheets of construction paper. For extra appeal, invite students to add paper scales to the dragon or attach crepe paper streamers for the dragon's breath. This intriguing display is an ideal way to highlight students' writing about dragons, the Chinese New Year, or Chinese culture.

新

年

快

樂

LANTERN

PLACE ON FOLD.

HANDLE

DOG

Those born under the dog sign are extremely honest. They have a deep sense of justice and duty and can always keep a secret.

1958, 1970, 1982, 1994, 2006, 2018

PIG

People born under this sign have a strong inner strength and are very brave. They are shy, courteous and make friends for life.

1959, 1971, 1983, 1995, 2007, 2019

RAT

People born under the sign of the Rat have great charm. They are known for their ambition, integrity and drive.

1960, 1972, 1984, 1996, 2008, 2020

OX

Ox people are very patient and are good listeners. They inspire others with their calm assuredness.

1961, 1973, 1985, 1997, 2009, 2021

TIGER

Tiger people are considered very good friends. They are careful planners and are respected by others.

1962, 1974, 1986, 1998, 2010, 2022

HARE

Persons born under the sign of the hare are blessed with good fortune and seldom lose their tempers. They always keep their promises.

1963, 1975, 1987, 1999, 2011, 2023

DRAGON

People born under the sign of the dragon have been given the gifts of courage, health, and gentleness. They are good rulers and sensitive to others.

1952, 1964, 1976, 1988, 2012, 2024

SNAKE

People born under this sign possess great wisdom. They are fortunate in money matters and are very handsome or beautiful.

1953, 1965, 1977, 1989, 2001, 2013

HORSE

Those born under the sign of the horse are very cheerful and popular with others. They are good with their hands and quite talented.

1954, 1966, 1978, 1990, 2002, 2014

RAM

People born under this sign are very artistic and enjoy beautiful things. They are most happy when doing creative tasks.

1955, 1967, 1979, 1991, 2003, 2015

MONKEY

Monkey people are good decision makers and have great common sense. They are quite successful and keep themselves well-informed.

1956, 1968, 1980, 1992, 2004, 2016

ROOSTER

People born under this sign are outspoken and deep thinkers. They are devoted to their work and attract loyal friends.

1957, 1969, 1981, 1993, 2005, 2017

DRAGON GAME

Finish

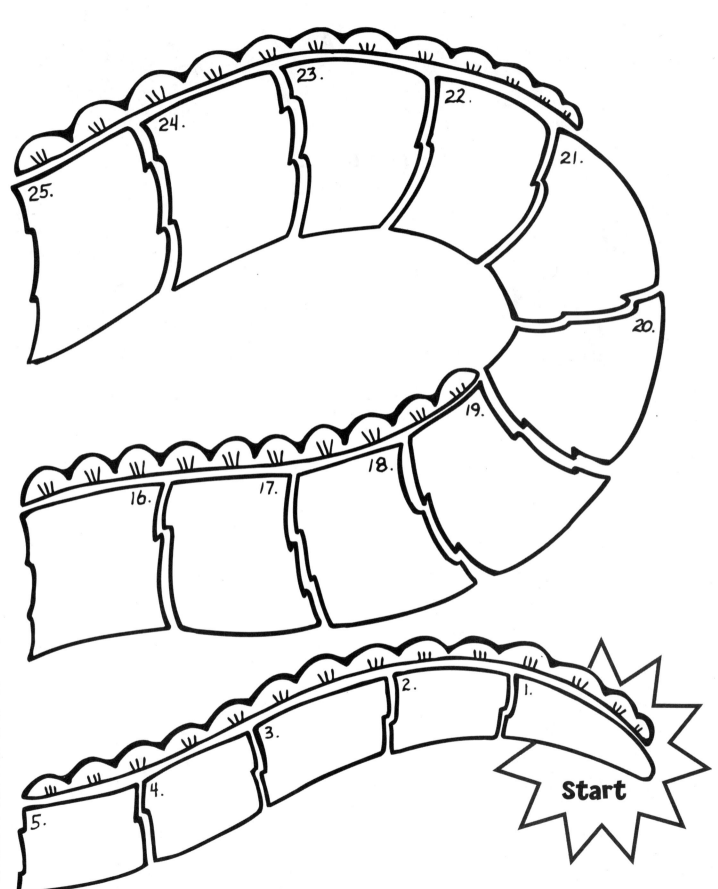

23.

24.

22.

25.

21.

20.

19.

16.

17.

18.

2.

1.

3.

4.

5.

Start

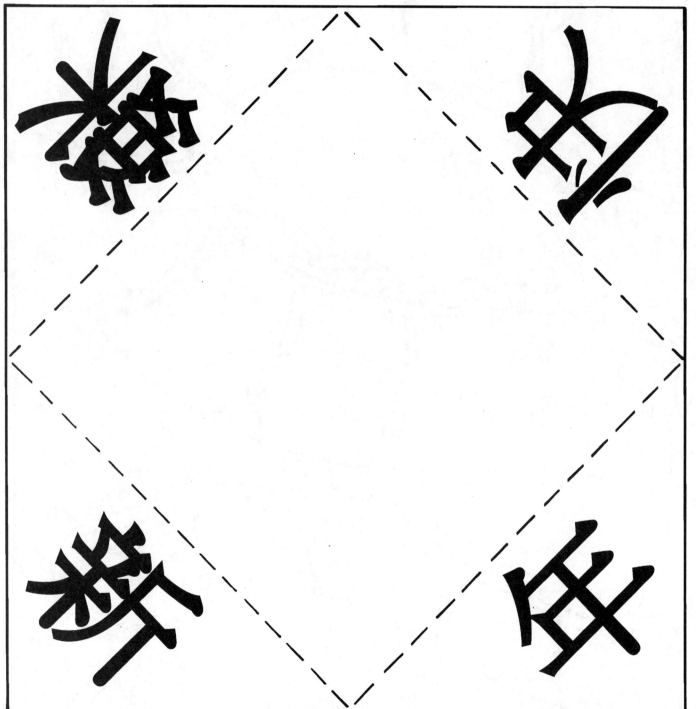

January Monthly Idea Book © Scholastic Teaching Resources

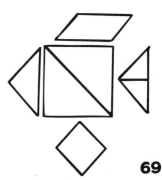

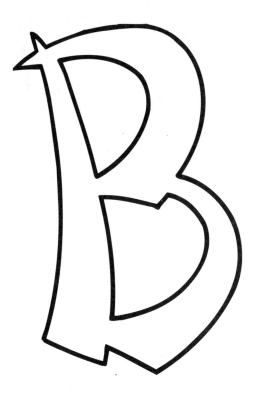
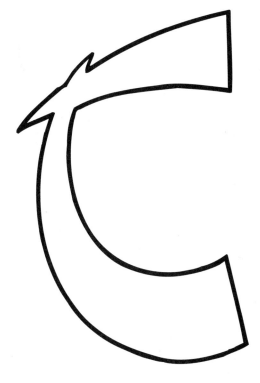

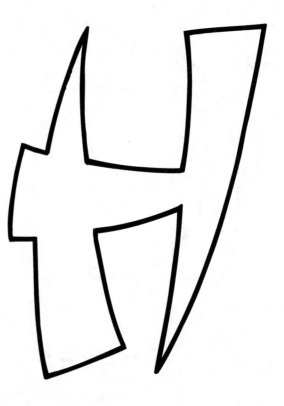

January Monthly-Idea Book© Scholastic Teaching Resources

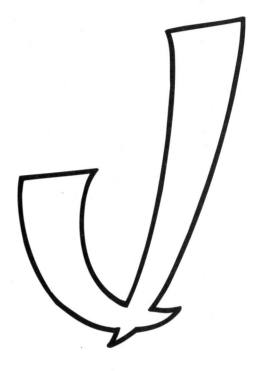

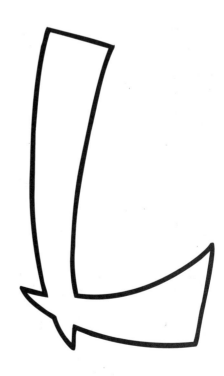

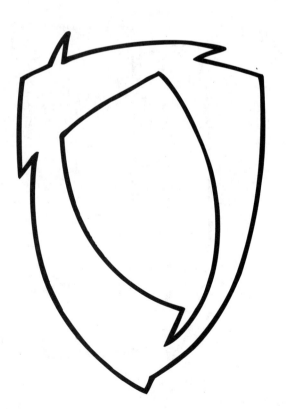

January Monthly Idea Book © Scholastic Teaching Resources

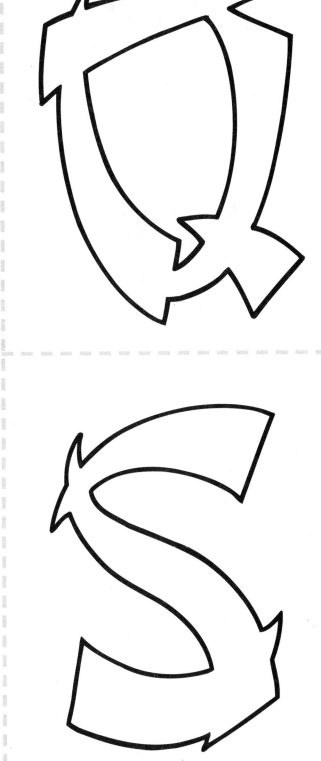

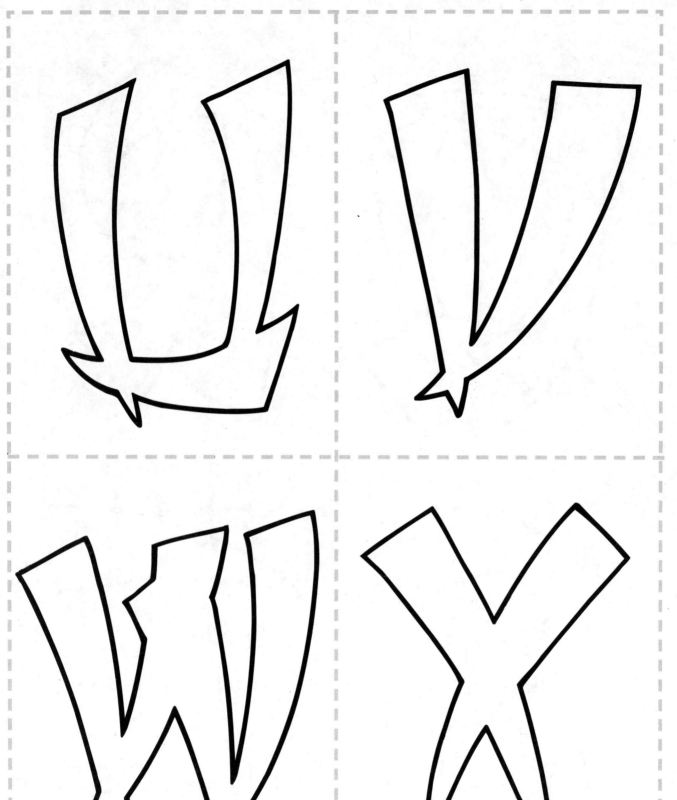

January Monthly Idea Book © Scholastic Teaching Resources

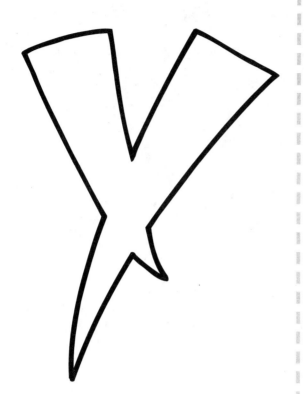

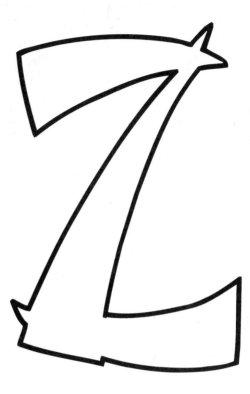

DR. MARTIN LUTHER KING, JR.

Martin Luther King, Jr., was born on January 15th, 1929 in Atlanta, Georgia. Ordained as a Baptist minister like his father before him, Dr. King accepted the pastorship of the Dexter Avenue Baptist Church in Montgomery, Alabama. In 1953, he married Coretta Scott, and together they raised four children.

During the 1950's, Dr. King became a leader in the Civil Rights Movement. Among his first challenges was the boycotting of segregated buses. Despite threats to his life, Dr. King stood fast in his convictions. He urged people to forgive their enemies and try to achieve peaceful solutions to their problems.

On August 28, 1963, Dr. King spoke to more than 250,000 people at a massive civil rights demonstration in front of the Lincoln Memorial in Washington, DC. He spoke of his hopes and "dreams" for the brotherhood of man. Here is one brief excerpt from that famous speech:

"I have a dream that my four little children will one day live in a nation where they will not be judged by the color of their skin but by the content of their character . . . ."

In 1964, Dr. King was awarded the Nobel Peace Prize for his work in using nonviolence as a means to overcome unfairness and discrimination. The same year, Dr. King was chosen by *TIME* magazine as its "Man of the Year."

Dr. King took part in many marches and peaceful demonstrations for the equality of all individuals. He also participated in major drives for black voter registration. By 1967, Dr. King had been arrested and jailed thirteen times. He was assassinated in 1968 in a motel in Memphis, Tennessee.

A dynamic leader in the Civil Rights Movement, few in the history of America have inspired the nation as Dr. King did.

Suggested Activities

★ CIVIL RIGHTS WORD FIND

Distribute a photocopy of page 86 to each student. Explain that the word bank on their page contains words associated with the Civil Rights Movement and that students should find and circle the same words in their puzzles. Later, students will use some of those words to write a paragraph about Dr. King.

After the activity page is complete, ask students to define each word. (They can turn their page over and record the definitions on the back.) Provide dictionaries and other resources for students to use for research.

To take vocabulary-building one step further, have the class brainstorm other words and phrases associated with Dr. King. Discuss each word and phrase in turn. Encourage students to share what knowledge they've gained about civil rights through books, movies, and other media. Record student responses on chart paper. As you continue to study Dr. King with the class, revisit the chart and add more information and details.

★ WELL-EARNED PEACE BADGES

Martin Luther King, Jr., had a dream that all men and women, and boys and girls, could live together in peace and harmony. He asked that we not judge one another by the color of our skin but by the content of our character. He also encouraged all people to solve their problems peaceably.

To reward students for seeking peaceful solutions to their own conflicts or disagreements, photocopy a class supply of the badge pattern on page 87. Then, as members of the class demonstrate examples of using peaceful solutions or exhibit acts of kindness, award badges to those students, writing words of praise on them or the specific method the students used to reach a solution. For example, you might award badges to students who settle a disagreement by reaching a compromise or who offer help to others having difficulty in their assignments. Students can color their badges with crayons or markers then affix double-sided tape to the back so they can proudly wear their badges or attach them to their bookbags. Or, you might display the badges on an incentive chart for all to see. The chart will motivate students and reward them for their efforts.

★ CALLS FOR CHANGE

Read to students a portion of the speech given by Dr. Martin Luther King, Jr., in Washington, DC, in 1963. Explain that Dr. King did not mean a dream such as the ones we have when we sleep, but rather a wish or hope.

Distribute a photocopy of page 88 to each student. Tell students that they can help make Dr. King's dream a reality at school and at home. Ask them to sign the pledge, promising to work harder at finding peaceful means to solving problems in the classroom, on the playground, and other places.

To underscore the importance of making a pledge, collect the sheets and bind them into a book. For a finishing touch, add a construction paper cover and have students decorate it.

★ MAKING DREAMS KNOWN

Introduce this activity by having students discuss the dream Dr. King had for our country. Explain that each student will be making a mobile using cloud patterns to record his or her own dream for the community, country, and world. Tell students that their dreams must be for the betterment of others (such as peace, health, and nutrition).

Distribute photocopies of pages 89–91 to each student, along with a 2-foot length of yarn, scissors, and a hole punch. To make the mobile, have students:

1. Cut out each pattern.

2. Record their dreams for their community, country, and the world on the corresponding patterns.

3. Punch one hole at the top of each smaller cloud and three holes at the bottom of the large cloud, where indicated.

4. Cut the yarn into four pieces of varying lengths. String a piece of yarn through each cloud (page 91) and then through a hole in the large cloud. Knot the ends of the yarn.

5. Punch a hole in the top of the biggest cloud and tie the last length of yarn to it.

When the dream mobiles are complete, hang them in the classroom or send them home with students to share with families.

★ WRITING ABOUT RESEARCH

Provide students with several photocopies of the stationery on page 93. Explain that students will research and write about Martin Luther King, Jr., or others like him. You might present the following topics for students to choose from:

- Dr. King's statement ". . . they will not be judged by the color of their skin but by the content of their character . . . "

- people who have demonstrated great courage and/or have risked their lives for freedom and justice (such as Harriet Tubman, Mohandas Gandhi, and Desmond Tutu)

- solving problems and disagreements without violence by developing a variety of nonviolent solutions to problematic scenarios (such as bullying, unfairness, teasing)

- other Nobel Peace Prize winners (Martin Luther King, Jr., was a recipient of the award in 1964) and the reasons they were chosen to receive the award

When students are ready to publish their writing, have them color and attach a photocopy of the book cover (page 92). Or, they can make a book cover of their own design to add some polish to the presentation of their work.

Civil Rights Word Find

Find these words in the puzzle below:

BOYCOTT   CHARACTER   DEMONSTRATION

EQUALITY   JUSTICE   OPPORTUNITY   PEACE

PREJUDICE   PROTEST   RIGHTS

```
E  Q  U  A  L  I  T  Y  K  M  J  N  H  G  A  S  W  E  R  T  X
A  S  W  D  V  F  R  T  F  V  G  E  S  E  D  F  T  G  H  Y  U
F  R  I  E  P  D  S  X  D  R  T  W  U  I  C  F  T  G  B  N  B
Q  E  S  D  E  R  G  T  G  H  N  Y  F  R  C  U  S  T  O  M  O
A  S  E  R  A  P  R  E  J  U  D  I  C  E  C  V  F  R  G  D  P
A  O  C  V  C  C  O  N  U  V  F  A  F  R  B  D  E  R  T  Y  P
X  L  C  D  E  M  O  N  S  T  R  A  T  I  O  N  T  P  N  Q  O
Q  U  B  O  Y  C  O  T  T  E  B  A  E  G  L  A  S  D  E  X  R
A  T  D  F  G  H  X  E  I  T  Y  H  C  H  L  E  B  R  A  T  T
Z  I  X  C  H  A  R  A  C  T  E  R  G  T  S  D  V  B  N  M  U
A  O  F  B  N  M  J  K  E  A  T  H  E  S  T  I  M  E  X  C  N
W  N  S  D  B  A  L  Z  W  O  N  S  C  D  R  E  T  G  H  Y  I
M  I  J  N  P  G  H  T  V  D  E  R  T  F  P  R  O  T  E  S  T
A  S  D  E  W  Q  X  C  V  J  A  N  U  X  Q  T  A  Z  I  M  Y
```

Using four of the words from the puzzle, write a paragraph about Martin Luther King, Jr. If you need more space, use the back of this page.

_____

_____

_____

January Monthly Idea Book © Scholastic Teaching Resources

I promise to work harder at finding peaceful solutions

to problems at home and at school.

I also promise not to judge other people unfairly

and to help make Dr. King's dream a reality.

_____   _____

Student's Signature   Date

January Monthly Idea Book © Scholastic Teaching Resources

Kevin

I have a dream . . .

. . . for my community!

. . . for my country!

_____

_____

_____

_____

. . . for the world!

_____

_____

_____

_____

Name

I have a dream . . .

Dr. Martin Luther King, Jr.

January Monthly Idea Book © Scholastic Teaching Resources

WINTRY WEATHER

You don't have to live where it snows to learn about winter weather! Many of the science-related activities in this unit can be easily accomplished with a freezer and some imagination. Other activities can be used in the classroom to reinforce a variety of skills, including winter-related vocabulary.

Suggested Activities

★ SNOWFLAKE PATTERNS

It is often difficult to observe real snowflakes because they melt so fast. But, by catching snowflakes on dark paper, students can make a quick study of the various shapes of snowflakes before they melt away. Before going outdoors on a snowy day, share these quick facts about snowflakes with students:

- Snowflakes are six-sided crystals.

- No two snowflakes are exactly alike.

- The size and shape of a snowflake is determined by the air temperature, moisture content, and the amount of time it has to grow before hitting a surface.

Next distribute black sheets of construction paper to students and head outdoors. As the snow falls, encourage students to catch a few flakes on their paper and then examine the crystals closely (without touching them). You might have them use magnifying glasses so they can view the crystallized shapes of their snowflakes more clearly. Back in the classroom, invite volunteers to share what they observed and describe the different snowflake patterns they encountered.

★ SNOWFLAKE IMPRINTS

Use this idea to make snow imprints that you can bring into the classroom for additional study. In advance, place several clear overhead transparencies in the freezer along with an equal number of cardboard pieces that have been trimmed to the size of the transparencies. Also, place a can of unscented hair spray (or clear artist's fixative) in the freezer. Then, during a light snowfall, invite students to go outdoors to catch snowflakes. Take along the transparencies, cardboard, and hair spray, keeping them as cold as possible while transporting them. Outdoors, clip each transparency to a piece of cardboard, and distribute to student pairs to use as snowflake catchers. As students catch their snowflakes, spray the crystals with a light coat of hairspray. Then set the sheets of captured snowflakes aside in a cold, sheltered area to dry—undisturbed—for a few hours. After the snowflakes melt and the water evaporates, imprints of the snowflakes will remain on the transparencies.

★ FREEZER CRYSTALS

Even if you live in an area where snowfall is rare or doesn't occur at all, students can still observe the crystal-like patterns of frost that accumulates in a freezer or on frozen-food packages. Or, have students freeze tiny drops of water to observe with magnifying glasses (or a microscope). If desired, share a book that features art of actual snowflakes, such as *Snowflakes in Photographs* by W. A. Bentley (Dover Publications, 2000). Students can compare their observations of frost to the snowflake photos and tell how the two are similar and different.

★ UNIQUE SNOWFLAKES

Invite students to design their own unique snowflakes! Make photocopies of the snowflake template on page 101 and distribute to students. Explain that even snowflakes that fall at the same time can look very different from each other. Then see how many different snowflake designs the class can make from their patterns. To make the snowflakes, have students do the following:

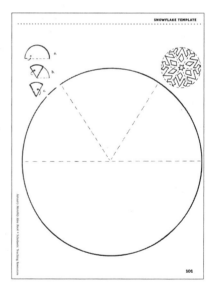

1. Cut out the circle and fold it in half. Fold it again in thirds, as shown.

a.

2. Cut out designs along both folded edges of the pie-shaped wedge and along the top curved edge.

b.

3. Unfold the wedge to reveal the snowflake pattern.

c.

WINTERTIME SCIENCE EXPERIMENTS

Extend students' learning about icy-weather topics with these ideas:

Ice Expands: What happens to water when it freezes? After students share their thoughts, conduct a simple experiment. First, fill a plastic container halfway with water. Mark the water level with a permanent marker or wax pencil. Then place the container in a freezer. After the water has frozen solid, remove the container and show it to students. Discuss the level of the water, explaining that water (a liquid) expands—or takes up more space—as it freezes into ice (a solid).

Salt Water: Ask students if they think salt water can freeze. After they respond, explain that salt water does freeze, but at a lower temperature than plain water. Point out that glaciers, icebergs, and polar caps in the oceans are made of salt water. Then invite volunteers to identify on a globe some areas of the earth where salt water might freeze in nature.

Traction: Explain that salt and sand are often used to make ice less slippery on sidewalks and roads. Then ask students to tell which they think provides the best traction (or grip): salt or sand. To test their responses, divide the class into small groups. Give two ice cubes to each group. Ask the groups to sprinkle salt on top of one ice cube and sand on the other. Have each group invert its ice cubes then slide them across a table. Which one has the best traction? Finally, have students place the ice cubes on a paper towel, sprinkle more salt and sand onto the appropriate cubes, and observe to see which one melts faster.

 ## MITTEN MATCH

Prepare a variety of matching activities to give students practice in developing skills, such as letter recognition, math facts, opposites, and words and their definitions. Simply photocopy and cut out a supply of the mitten patterns on page 102. Then, on each pair, record the words, images, or math facts you'd like students to match. They can match the mitten pairs, then attach them to a clothesline in the classroom.

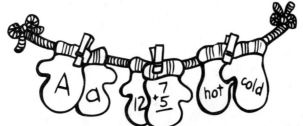

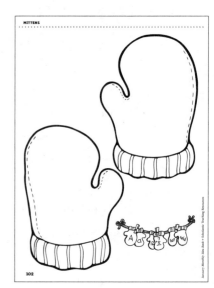

★ WINTRY WORD FIND

Discuss the role that the water cycle plays in the formation of wintry weather. Also, talk about the different forms that frozen water can take, such as frost, snow, and icicles. Then, to further expand and reinforce students' wintry weather vocabulary, have them complete the word find on page 103. After they have searched for all of the words listed in the word bank and circled them in the puzzle, have students use some of the words in the context of their own writing. That's one way to make vocabulary words stick!

★ LET'S MAKE A SNOWMAN!

Use the snowman patterns (pages 104-105) to motivate and reward students for their efforts in class. To prepare, photocopy a supply of the patterns, and cut loosely around each one. Then explain that you will award one pattern piece at a time to students as they complete assignments or meet an established goal.

Start by distributing the bottom piece of the snowman to students. Then distribute the other pieces in this order as students earn them: the middle section with arms, head, scarf, hat, mittens (one at a time, if desired), broom, and carrot nose. Once a student has collected all of the pieces, ask him or her to cut out the patterns and glue them onto a sheet of dark construction paper to make the snowman. Students can then use crayons or markers to add jolly faces and other details. Display the completed snowmen on a class bulletin board.

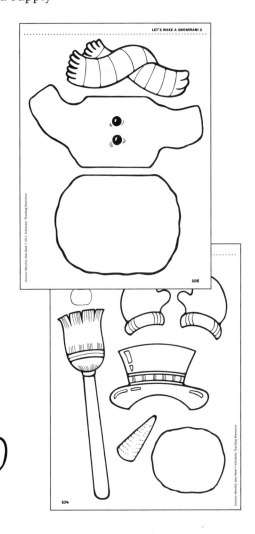

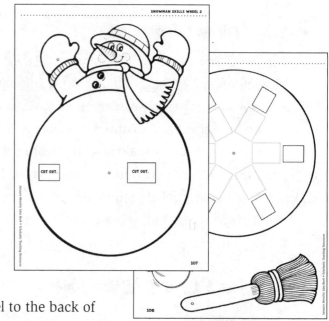

 SNOWMAN SKILLS WHEEL

Reinforce developing skills with this winter-themed learning tool. To get started, provide students with tagboard photocopies of the patterns on pages 106–107, two brass fasteners, and scissors. To assemble the wheel, have students do the following:

1. Cut out each pattern.

2. Cut out the two rectangular windows on the snowman. (Younger students may need help with this.)

3. Use a brass fastener to attach the wheel to the back of the snowman, as shown.

4. Use a brass fastener to attach the broom to the snowman's right mitten where indicated.

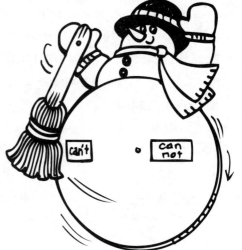

To program their wheels, have students fill in math problems and answers, contractions and their two-word counterparts, or other skills you are targeting by turning the wheel and writing in the boxes behind the window cutouts. When finished, show students how to read the problem through the window on the right side of the wheel and then check their response by moving the broom on the left.

 A JOLLY PAGE TOPPER

Celebrate student achievement with snowman page toppers that will make any bulletin board a hit. Make photocopies of the pattern on page 108. To make each topper, cut out the pattern along the solid lines. Fold along the dotted lines, tape the back together, and slip over the corner of a student's work. For added flare, make the photocopies on color paper, or use glitter glue to add details to the snowman.

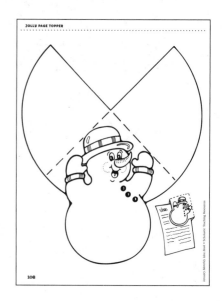

★ SNOWMAN MOBILE

Whether the class is studying winter weather or just getting into the spirit of the winter season, these mobiles are easy to make and fun to display. To get started, distribute photocopies of page 109 to students, along with two 1-foot lengths of yarn, scissors, and a hole punch. To make the mobile, tell students to:

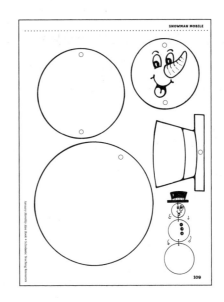

1. Cut out the snowman patterns.

2. Punch holes, where indicated, in each of the patterns.

3. Cut a 1-foot length of yarn into three shorter pieces of varying lengths. Then string the pieces of yarn through the holes in the patterns, as shown, and knot the ends.

4. Attach the remaining 1-foot length of yarn to the top of the hat to make a hanger.

The completed mobile will have lengths of yarn connecting parts of the snowman in this order, from top to bottom: top hat, head, midsection (medium-size circle), and bottom (large circle). Invite students to draw additional features on their snowman. Then hang the mobiles in the classroom or send them home with students to enjoy with their families.

★ WINTER FUN PICTURE CARDS

Make photocopies of the cards on pages 110–111. Cut out the cards and use them as nametags, calendar symbols, patterning practice, or matching activities.

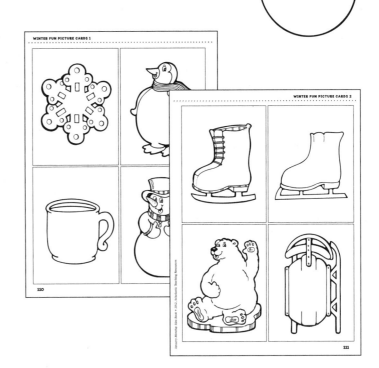

SNOWY STORY STARTERS

Encourage students to write creative winter tales with descriptive words, such as:

avalanche	hibernate
blizzard	icicles
freeze	shiver
frostbite	snowdrift
glacier	snowmobile

Or, try these suggestions for story starters:

■ *Hockey players were skating too close to thin ice when the unthinkable happened.*

■ *Oh, no! I lost my mittens again!*

■ *No one was expecting the ski lift to stop halfway up the mountain.*

■ *Snow fell for eight straight days.*

■ *The day it snowed on the Fourth of July . . .*

■ *The winner of the race receives a pair of magic . . .*

■ *When we started building the biggest snowman ever . . .*

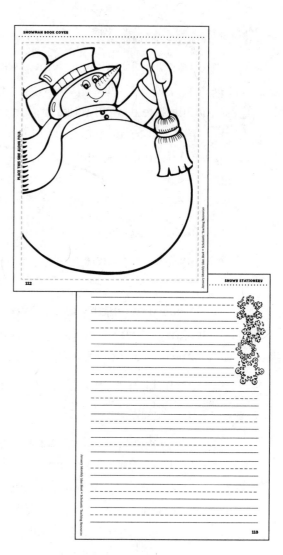

To provide students with stationery that will make their writing sparkle, distribute copies of the snow-themed stationery on page 113. When they are finished editing and are ready to publish their writing, offer students photocopies of the book cover on page 112 to use with their final copy. Have them add a title and author line to the cover. Then invite volunteers to share their wintry writing with the class.

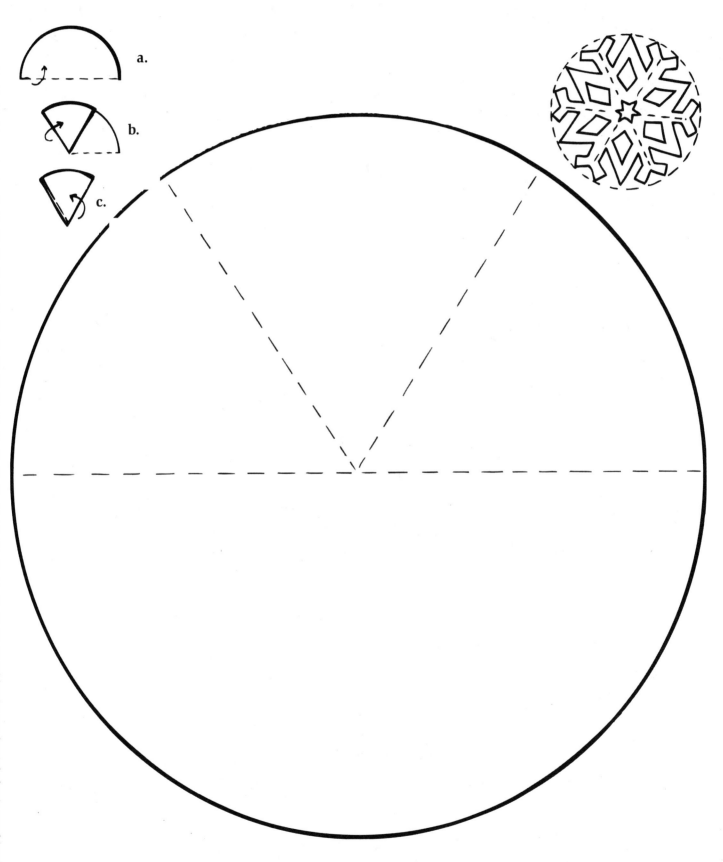

a.

b.

c.

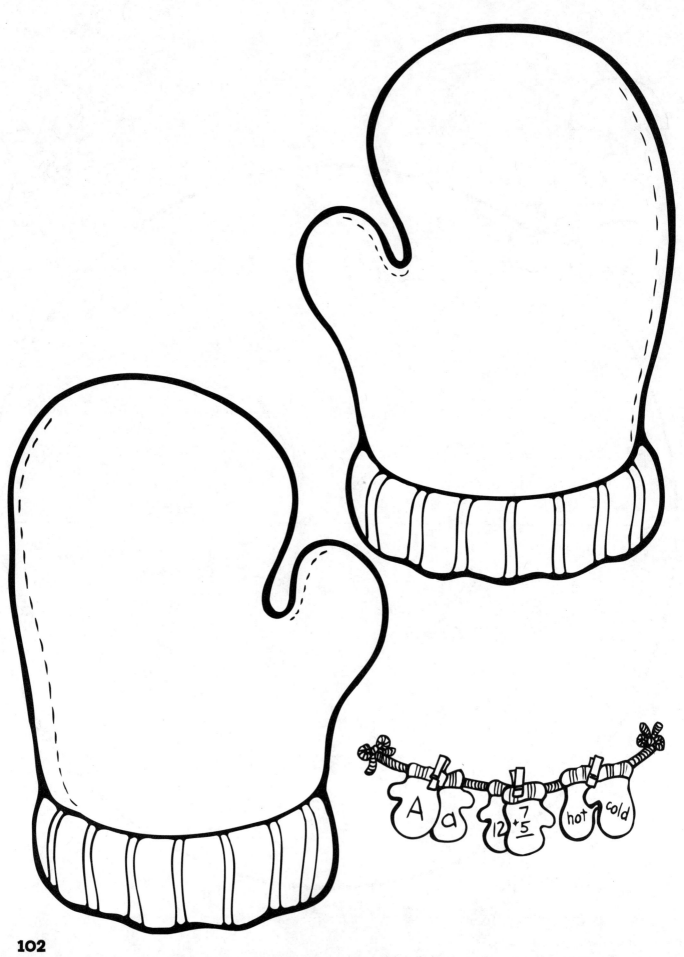

Wintry Word Find

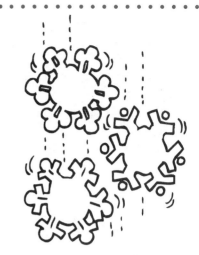

Find these words in the puzzle below:

CONDENSATION   CLOUD   CRYSTAL   FROST

ICICLE   MOISTURE   PRECIPITATION   SNOW

SNOWFLAKE   SNOWMAN   STORM   WINTER

```
G N M K L O P L K M J N H G A S W E R T X
A S W D V F R T F V G E S E D F T G H Y U
F R I E S N O W F L A K E I C F T G B N B
Q E S D N R G T G H N Y F R C U S W O M O
A S F R O S T E C U D I C E C V M I G D P
A O C V W P R E C I P I T A T I O N T Y T
X L C D M M O N R T R A T I O N I T N Q P
Q U B O A C O T Y E S A E S L A S E E X R
A T C O N D E N S A T I O N L E T R A T T
Z I L C H A R A T T O C G O S D U B N M U
A O O B N M J K A A R I E W T I R E X C S
W N U D B A L Z L O M C C D R E E G H Y I
M I D N P G H T V D E L T F P A O T K S C
A S D E W Q X C V J A E U E D U P L L T Y
```

Using six of the words from the puzzle, write about what you have learned about wintry weather. If you need more space, use the back of this page.

_____

_____

_____

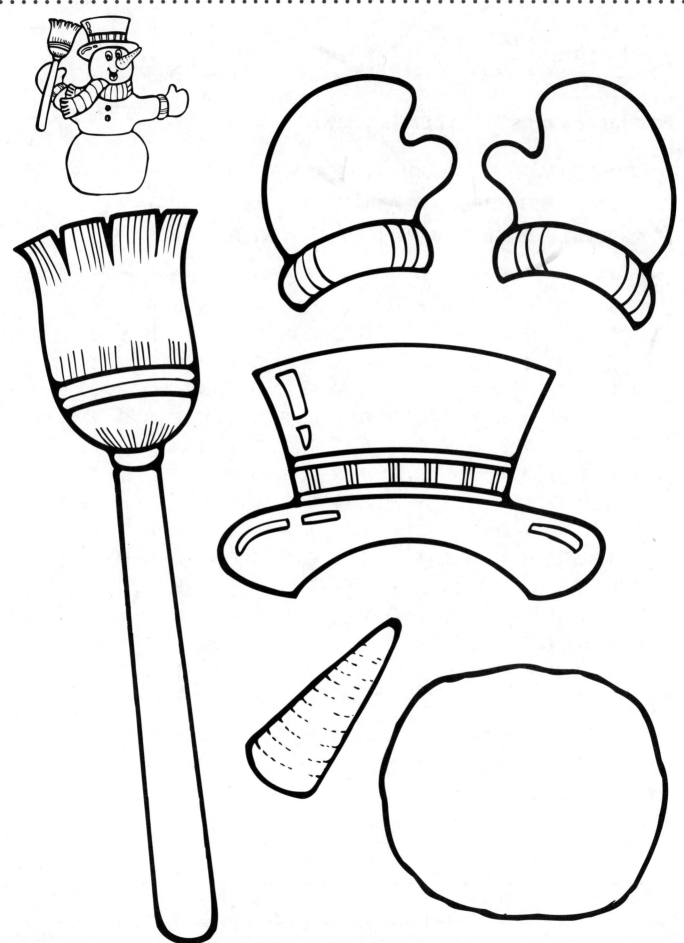

can't

can
not

January Monthly Idea Book © Scholastic Teaching Resources

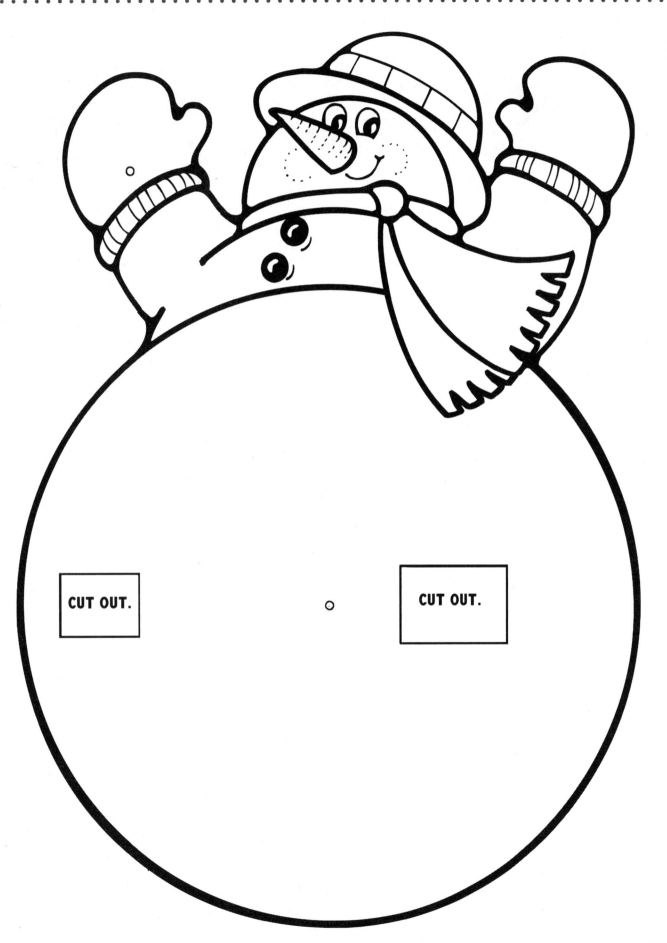

CUT OUT.

CUT OUT.

Jose

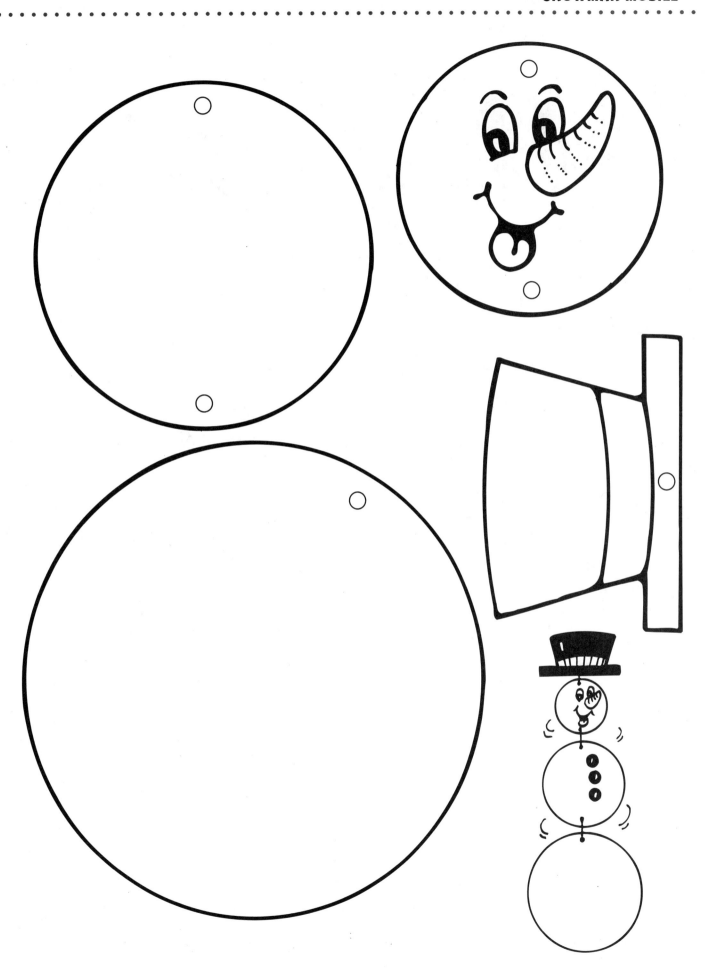

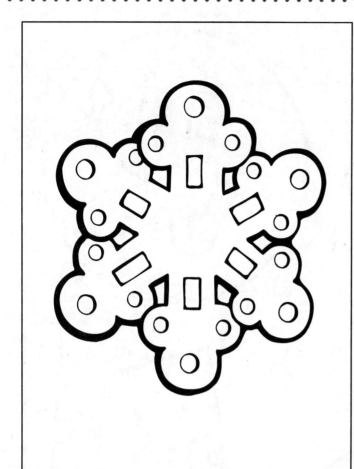

January Monthly Idea Book © Scholastic Teaching Resources

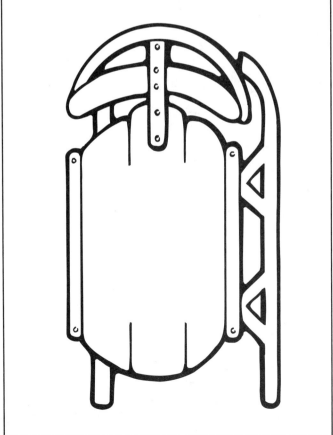

PLACE THIS SIDE ALONG FOLD.

January Monthly Idea Book © Scholastic Teaching Resources

THE ARCTIC AND ANTARCTIC

Studying the poles will likely be new for many students. Distribute copies of the maps (pages 120–121) to use as a springboard for a discussion about the geography of the Polar Regions.

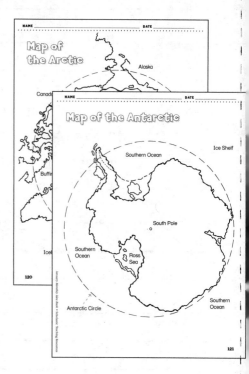

Only the most intrepid travelers have ventured to the Arctic or Antarctic. Following is a brief timeline of notable polar explorers and their achievements:

- In 1909, navy commander Robert E. Peary and his crew were the first to reach the North Pole.

- In 1911, a Norwegian explorer named Ronald Amundsen became the first person to reach the South Pole.

- In 1914, Ernest Shackleton and the crew of the *Endurance* set out to cross the continent of Antarctica. Their expedition became an epic journey of survival and extraordinary bravery.

- In 1929, naval officer Richard E. Byrd was the first pilot to fly over the South Pole. He later led expeditions for the United States government.

- In 1958, the U.S. submarine, *USS Nautilus,* traveled under the Arctic icecap, covering a distance of nearly 2,000 miles.

- In 1978, a Japanese explorer named Naomi Uemura made the first solo dog sled trip to the North Pole.

Suggested Activities

GEOGRAPHY WITH ORANGES

Increase students' familiarity with the concept of hemispheres by discussing the abstract in a concrete way. First, distribute navel oranges to students, telling them that they will use the oranges to make a globe. Then, using an actual globe, show students the line that represents the earth's equator. Point out that the area below the equator is referred to as the Southern Hemisphere and the area above is the Northern Hemisphere. Then instruct students to use pens to mark and label the equator on their "globe" oranges. Have them label other areas on their globes as well, such as the Arctic, Antarctic, the North and South Poles, and surrounding oceans. Finally, invite students to peel their oranges and enjoy a refreshing treat.

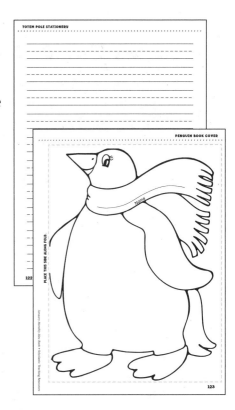

EXPEDITIONS TO THE POLES

Older students can be encouraged to research the lives of the people that risked it all to reach the North and South Poles. Invite students to locate the explorers' routes on the maps on pages 120 and 121. For an extra challenge, ask groups to find out more about Martin Frobisher, Samuel Hearne, Sir John Franklin, and Nils A. E. Nordenskjold. These men were just a few of the many explorers who have attempted to find water routes through the frozen northern seas. When students are ready to publish their research, invite them to compile their findings into books as a record of their learning. Students can use the stationery (page 122) for their final copy and then bind their pages behind a copy of the book cover (page 123). To complete their book, have students add a title and author line to their book cover.

ADDING CHILLY DETAILS

Divide the class into two groups. Explain that one group will research details about the Arctic, while the other studies the Antarctic. To help students learn about the geography of their region, distribute photocopies of the maps (pages 120 and 121) to the appropriate groups and ask them to label important or interesting areas on them. Also, instruct students to add a map key as a guide for interpreting the pictures, symbols, or colors that they use on their map. Younger students can add colorful details that differentiate land from water.

Make it clear that each group is responsible for teaching the other group about their particular Polar Region. In addition to geographical information, older students can choose to research topics such as the people or animals that live in their region of study.

COLD-WEATHER WORD FINDS

Complement your lessons with the word finds on pages 124 and 125. Invite students to search the puzzles to find words related to the Arctic and Antarctic. Then have them write a paragraph, as directed at the bottom of each puzzle page, using words from the word find. This activity will give students some much-needed practice with spelling and using the words in their own writing.

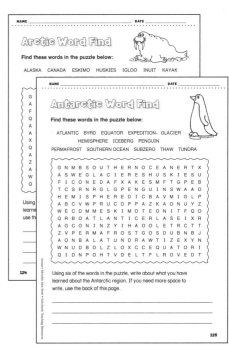

★ SNOW FLURRY FLASH CARDS

Reinforce whatever your students are learning with flash cards that fit the theme of this unit. Simply photocopy the cards (page 126) onto tagboard and cut them apart. You can program the back of the cards for use as flash cards to teach:

- ■ letters and numbers

- ■ math facts

- ■ content-area vocabulary words

- ■ sight words

The cards are ideal for learning-center activities, but you might also use them to label job charts, group students, and more. To store, just put them in a resealable plastic bag.

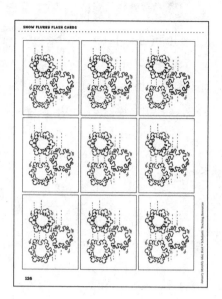

★ INDIGENOUS PEOPLES, THEN AND NOW

For thousands of years people have lived in the cold northern areas of North America and Asia. Their ingenuity helped them build homes, find food, develop transportation, and create appropriate clothing for the harsh climates. While some traditional practices in industry, food production, and fashion have been modernized, various peoples indigenous to the Arctic region still maintain their cultural traditions and ways of life.

Divide the class into several groups. Explain that each group will research different aspects of Eskimo or Inuit life and then present their findings to the class. Assign one topic (such as tribes, food, clothing, shelter, industry, art, or transportation) to each group to research. Students can use books available in the classroom as well as library books, Internet resources, and other sources such as videos and personal interviews for their research. Tell groups that they should look for information about life as an Eskimo or Inuit, both in the past and today, to compare how the indigenous peoples in the Arctic have

changed (or not) with the times. Younger students will enjoy hearing you read aloud from level-appropriate books on their topic. Afterward, they can discuss the information and then write and/or draw about what they have learned.

Most students will need a few days to complete their research for this assignment. To help groups prepare their presentations, provide copies of the puppet patterns and picture props on pages 127–130. Invite students to color and embellish the puppets or props of their choice to show what they've learned about a particular topic. In addition, you might invite groups to draw pictures and make models of items related to their topic. This will add interest to their presentations and help each member of the group shine!

★ WALRUS PUPPET PERFORMANCES

Did you know that walruses use their sensitive whiskers to sift through the seabed's floor to find dinner, including clams, starfish, and sea urchins? Or, that they use their large tusks for self-defense as well as to pull themselves up onto ice? An amazing creature, the walrus can even use its rock-hard skull as a battering ram to break through ice, a key skill for creating breathing holes when the cold water crusts with ice.

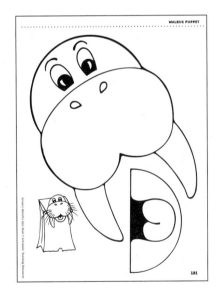

Send home photocopies of the walrus puppet patterns (page 131). Explain that students should find out surprising facts about walruses as homework. They can interview family members, read books, and do other research to unearth their information. Primed with their fun facts, students can make their puppet at home and practice telling family members what they have learned. Back at school, invite students to take turns performing with their puppets to share their findings with the class. (Most students will need a few days to complete this assignment.)

★ BEAR-PAW FACTS

Showcase the math and other learning that's happening in your classroom! Make and cut out photocopies of the bear paw patterns on page 132. Write math facts on the cutouts and put them in a learning center for students to practice basic facts. You might also write words of praise and encouragement on the paws, then display them with student work. Following are some additional ways to use the patterns.

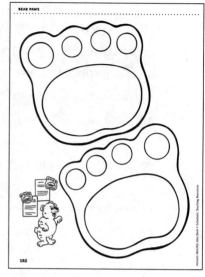

Arctic Animal Facts

Have students label the paw cutouts with facts about their favorite cold climate animals. But don't stop there! Help students connect those factoids to their own lives. Have them draw pictures to make their learning relevant. For example, a child who records how much a walrus weighs could draw a walrus next to a small car and display the drawing with the bear paw. (A small car weighs as much as a walrus and shares approximately the same length.) For starters, here's a fact you can share with students: A male walrus can grow over 12 feet in length and weigh as much as 3,500 pounds!.

True or False?

Label a supply of the paw cutouts with different statements about the geography, indigenous peoples, or animals native to the Polar Regions. Include a variety of statements that are both true and false. If desired, label the back of each paw with "True" or "False." Then invite volunteers to read the statements to the class. Challenge students to discuss and decide whether each statement is true or false before checking the answer.

★ POLAR INHABITANTS

Life at the poles is extreme, but the people and animals that inhabit those areas are well equipped for the challenges. Collect a number of resource books about polar animals from the school library and ask students to choose an animal to research (such as caribou, fox, hare, and wolf). Additional animals that live in these regions include a variety of whales, birds, and fish.

Several species of seals can be found at the poles, too, such as harbor seals, fur seals, and leopard seals. Seals are a favorite food of polar bears and killer whales, but their natural enemies also include sharks and man. Ask students to find out more about seals to share with the class. For instance, fur seals have

the ability to stay under water for long periods of time. But what happens when they emerge for a long-awaited breath?

When students have completed their research, display their work using the polar bear page framer (page 133). To make, cut out and attach the patterns to the edges of a 9- by 12-inch sheet of white construction paper. Then affix a student's work to the polar bear's "body" and display on a bulletin board or wall.

★ PENGUINS ON PARADE

Penguins live in a variety of places in the Southern Hemisphere. Though only found in this part of the world, some penguins aren't fond of ice and snow. In fact, some prefer warmer climates, such as the shores of South Africa or the islands of the Galapagos.

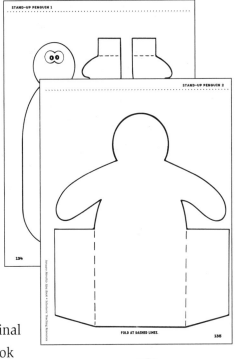

To help students learn about different types of penguins, have the class brainstorm what they have learned from books, movies, documentaries, and so on. Then group students and have each group research a particular breed of penguin and what makes that breed different from other types of penguins. You might have students begin their research by looking up penguins such as the Adelie, Magellanic, and Rockhopper. Students will find lots of information on websites for children's museums, at their local library, or by visiting an aquarium, if one is close by.

When groups are ready to present their findings, ask the students to write collaborative reports using what they learned about their particular type of penguin. They might write their final copy on the stationery (page 122) and bind the pages to the book cover (page 123).

You might also invite them to make stand-up penguins to use as props during their presentation. Simply distribute copies of the penguin patterns (pages 134–135) for students to color and cut out. Have them glue the body to the penguin base, fold the beak and feet along the lines, and glue those pieces to the base, as shown. Finally, demonstrate how to fold back the two sides of the base to stand the penguin on a flat surface. If desired, provide assorted craft materials (such as adhesive felt, feathers, and wiggle eyes) for students to use to enhance their penguin. After students complete their presentations, you might stand the penguins on a windowsill or bookshelf to create a parade of penguins!

Map of the Arctic

Alaska

Canada

Arctic Ocean

North Pole

○

Russia

Buffin Bay

Greenland

Barents Sea

Arctic Circle

Norway

Iceland

January Monthly Idea Book © Scholastic Teaching Resources

Map of the Antarctic

Ice Shelf

Southern Ocean

South Pole
o

Southern
Ocean

Ross
Sea

Southern
Ocean

Antarctic Circle

PLACE THIS SIDE ALONG FOLD.

Name

Arctic Word Find

Find these words in the puzzle below:

ALASKA   CANADA   ESKIMO   HUSKIES   IGLOO   INUIT   KAYAK

PARKA   POLAR BEAR   SEAL   UMIAK   WALRUS

```
G N M B L O P L K M J N H G A S W E R T X
A S W G V F R W F V G E S H U S K I E S U
F R C A N A D A F L A K E I M F T G B E B
Q U S P N R G L G H N I N U I T S W O A O
A S F R O S T R C U D I C E A V M I G L P
A O C V W P R U C I P P A R K A O N T Y Z
X L C D M M E S K I M O T I O N I T N Q O
Q A B O A C O T A E S K E S L A S E E X R
A T C O N I N Z Y T H R O N L E T I A T T
Z V L C H G R A A T O A G O S D U G N M J
A O N B A L A S K A R I E W T I Z L X C N
W N U D B O L Z L O X C C D R E E O H Y I
Q I D N P O L A R B E A R F L R O O E R T
```

Using six of the words in the puzzle, write about what you have learned about the Arctic region. If you need more space to write, use the back of this page.

_____

_____

_____

_____

January Monthly Idea Book ©Scholastic Teaching Resources

Antarctic Word Find

Find these words in the puzzle below:

ATLANTIC   BYRD   EQUATOR   EXPEDITION   GLACIER

HEMISPHERE   ICEBERG   PENGUIN

PERMAFROST   SOUTHERN OCEAN   SUBZERO   THAW   TUNDRA

```
G N M B S O U T H E R N O C E A N E R T X
A S W E G L A C I E R E S H U S K I E S U
F I C O N E D A F X A K E S M F T G P E B
T C S R N R G L G P E N G U I N S W A A O
H E M I S P H E R E D I C B A V M I G L P
A B C V W P R U C D P P A Z K A O N U Y Z
W E C D M M E S K I M O T E O N I T F Q O
Q R B O A T L A N T I C E R L A S E I X R
A G C O N I N Z Y I H A O O L E T R C T T
Z V P E R M A F R O S T G O S D U B N B J
A O N B A L A T U N D R A W T I Z E X Y N
W N U D B O L Z L O X C C E Q U A T O R I
Q I D N P O H T V D E L T F L R O V E D T
```

Using six of the words in the puzzle, write about what you have
learned about the Antarctic region. If you need more space to
write, use the back of this page.

_____

_____

_____

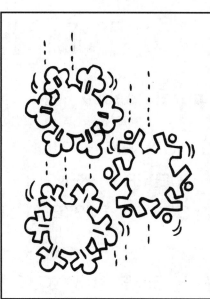

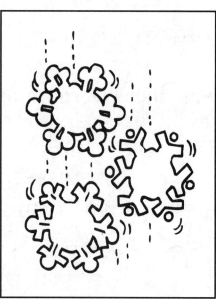

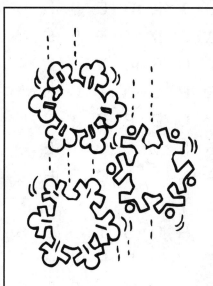

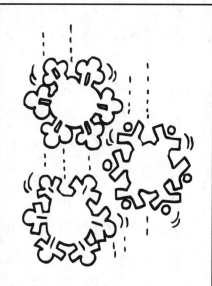

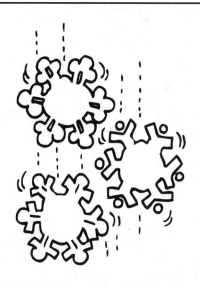

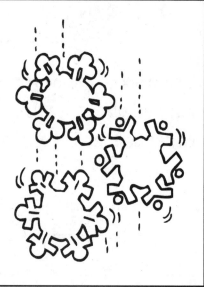

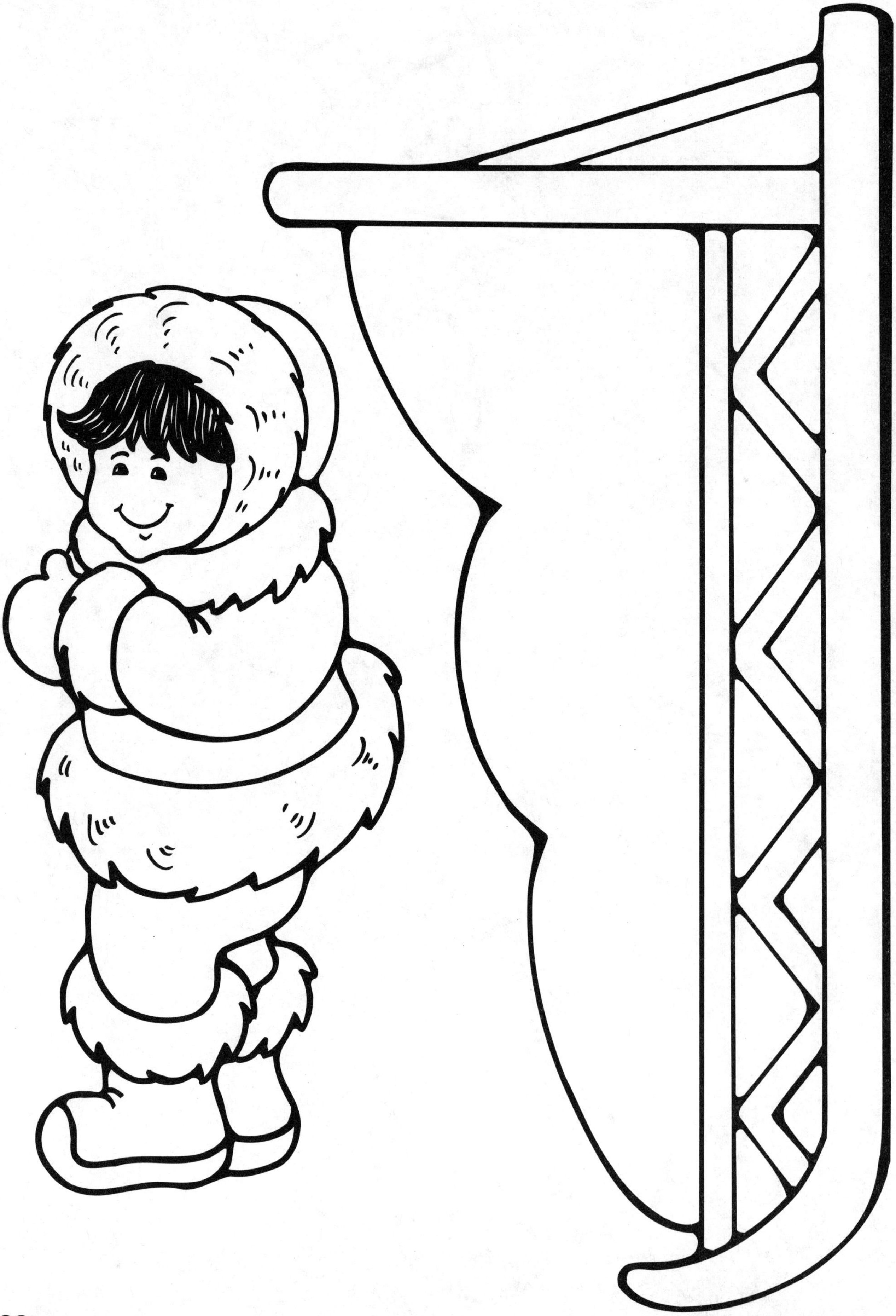

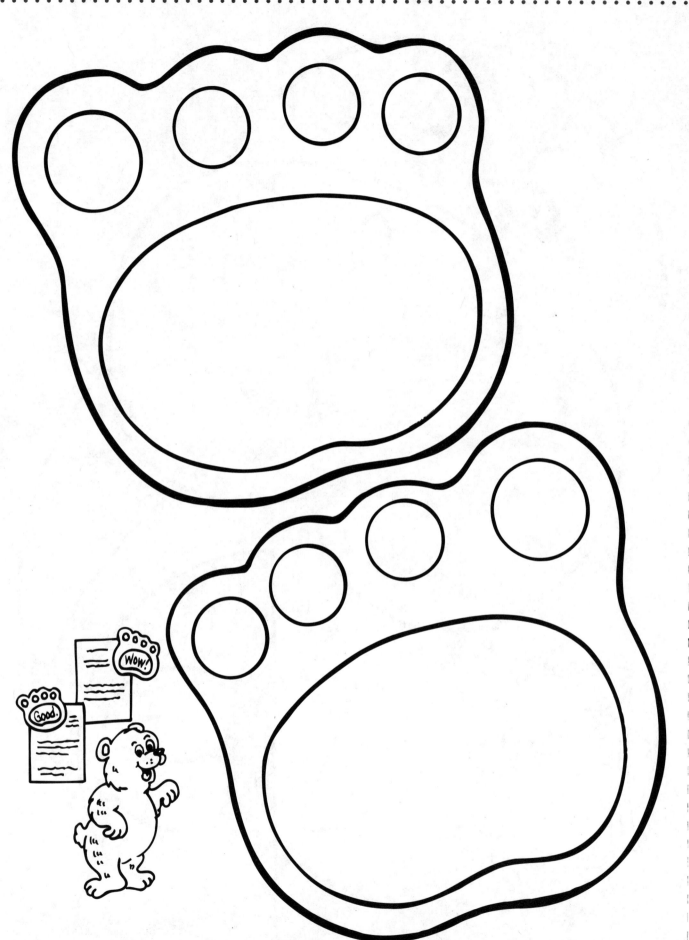

FOLD AT DASHED LINES.

AWARDS, INCENTIVES, AND MORE

Getting Started

Make several photocopies of the reproducibles on pages 138 through 142. Giving out the bookmarks, pencil toppers, notes, and certificates will show students your enthusiasm for their efforts and achievements. Plus, bookmarks and pencil toppers are a fun treat for students celebrating birthdays.

- Provide materials for decorating, including markers, color pencils, and stickers.

- Encourage students to bring home their creations to share and celebrate with family members.

★ BOOKMARKS

1. Photocopy onto tagboard and cut apart.

2. For more fanfare, punch a hole on one end and tie on a length of colorful ribbon or yarn.

★ PENCIL TOPPERS

1. Photocopy onto tagboard and cut out.

2. Use an art knife to cut through the Xs.

3. Slide a pencil through the Xs as shown.

★ SEND-HOME NOTES

1. Photocopy and cut apart.

2. Record the child's name and the date.

3. Add your signature.

4. Add more details about the student's day on the back of the note.

★ CERTIFICATES

1. Photocopy.

2. Record the child's name and other information, as directed.

3. Add details about the child's achievement (if applicable), then add your signature and the date.

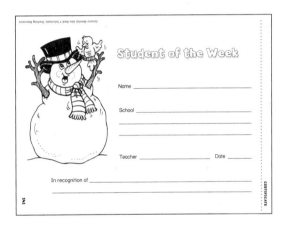

Warm up with a good book!

Visit the library!

Don't sleep all winter.

At the library . . .

. . . discover the wonders of winter!

Shawn!

_____
Name

was an enthusiastic learner!

_____
Date

_____
Teacher

_____
Name

did a terrific job!

_____
Date

_____
Teacher

_____
Name

showed a lot of effort!

_____
Date

_____
Teacher

_____
Name

was a big help!

_____
Date

_____
Teacher

Student of the Week

Name

School

Date

Teacher

In recognition of

January Monthly Idea Book © Scholastic Teaching Resources

Certificate of Achievement

presented to

Name

in recognition of

Teacher

Date

January Monthly Idea Book © Scholastic Teaching Resources

A New Year's Word Find, page 32

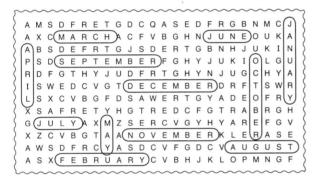

Months-of-the-Year Word Find, page 33

Unscramble the letters to spell the months of the year.

BDREECEM __December__   NEUJ __June__

TEROOCB __October__   RLPAI __April__

RYUABRFE __February__   TUUSGA __August__

VMEONREB __November__   AMY __May__

UYNJAAR __January__   CMRAH __March__

PMEESRBET __September__   LJYU __July__

Civil Rights Word Find, page 86

Wintry Word Find, page 103

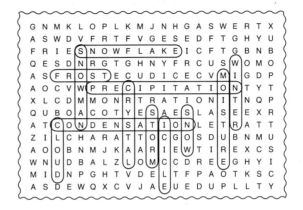

Arctic Word Find, page 124

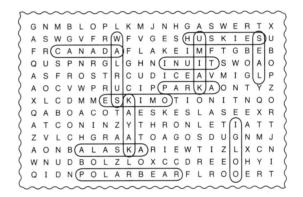

Antarctic Word Find, page 125

NOTES